D1330024

THE JOHN HARVARD LIBRARY

Howard Mumford Jones
Editor-in-Chief

CRUMBLING IDOLS

*Twelve Essays on Art
Dealing Chiefly With Literature
Painting and the Drama*

By

HAMLIN GARLAND

Edited by Jane Johnson

THE BELKNAP PRESS OF
HARVARD UNIVERSITY PRESS
Cambridge, Massachusetts
1960

PS1732
.C7
1960

© Copyright 1960 by the President and Fellows of Harvard College

Library of Congress Catalog Card Number 60–7994

Printed in the United States of America

*This book
is dedicated by the publishers to the memory of
Maurice Smith, A.B. 1919, LL.B. 1921, member of the Overseers' Com-
mittee to visit Harvard University Press from 1941 to 1958, and during
that time a constant and devoted worker in behalf of the Press
and The John Harvard Library.*

157140

CONTENTS

INTRODUCTION

In the spring of 1894 two Harvard undergraduates who had lately formed the publishing house of Stone and Kimball brought out a slim volume of essays entitled *Crumbling Idols*. The author was Hamlin Garland (1860–1940), a serious young man with fiery eyes and a bushy beard who looked every inch the radical. A native of Wisconsin, Garland had spent his youth in the West. In his twenties he went to New England where, after a year of avid, if unsystematic, self-education in the Boston Public Library, he entered upon a career of writing and lecturing upon literature and art. By 1894 he had published several novels as well as a distinguished collection of short stories, *Main Travelled Roads* (1891). With the publication of *Crumbling Idols*, Garland made his first — and only — major contribution to literary theory.

In 1895, describing this "little book on literary topics," a reviewer for the *Atlantic Monthly* noted that the manner of its manufacture "bore the marks of a dilettante taste in book-making. Its title page was printed in black and red, its paper simulated the sort known as English hand-made, the edges were deckle, and the types at the end of each essay ran off in an ornamental cue." But, he continued with elaborate amusement, the "precious" appearance of the volume was "quite at variance with its contents. To harmonize with them, the book should have been printed on birch bark and bound in butternut homespun, and should have had for cover design a dynamite bomb, say, with spluttering fire-tipped fuse; for the essays it contained were so many explosions of literary Jingoism and anarchy." [1] The reviewer, with his sharp eye for incongruity, would have been yet more amused if he could have contrasted the author's jaunty proclamations of Western superiority with the humble reverence for Eastern "culture" which had drawn Garland from Dakota to Boston a decade before. Yet in remarking a misalliance between the roughshod message of *Crumbling Idols* and its elegant binding (which Garland especially admired), the *Atlantic* critic raised an issue that has troubled students ever since. Was Garland a faithful son of the Middle Border, dedicated to its causes and sensitive to its trials, or a literary *parvenu* seeking acceptance in the East, who irresponsibly adopted reigning standards of taste? To put the matter crassly — did he want to record reality or merely to make money?

Of all American writers, it would seem that Garland should be the last whose motives might be debated. Few authors have published a more extensive record of their lives than is contained in Garland's two tetralogies: the Middle Border series, which is a history of his family, and the volumes of his "literary log." Yet critics, finding that he "declined from realism," have questioned his personal integrity, accused him of subservience to influential editors like Richard Watson Gilder of the *Century Magazine*, and discovered disillusionment or psychic compensation in his later work. There is some truth in these interpretations, but Garland's career need not seem enigmatic if we agree

[1] "New Figures in Literature and Art," *Atlantic Monthly*, LXXVI (Dec. 1895), 842.

that for him personal integrity and financial success were not incompatible. There is ample testimony to Garland's highmindedness. Edwin Markham, for instance, described him as a man "you could not think of as engaging in any selfish intrigues." [2] Yet Garland was always frankly interested in economic success. He never failed to point out that realism was remunerative: Chapter III of *Crumbling Idols*, "The Question of Success," is an instance in point. Late in life he still recalled his youthful envy of Alice French, who could command "three hundred dollars for a story of six thousand words . . . when I was glad to get thirty for mine." [3]

Crumbling Idols offers clues to both Garland's conception of realism and his feeling for the Middle Border. Though the essays in this volume were rewritten after Garland went to Chicago in 1893, a great part of *Crumbling Idols* first appeared in articles published by two eastern magazines, the *Arena* of Boston and the *Forum* of New York. Both these journals were "liberal" in outlook, representing what the *Arena* editor, B. O. Flower, liked to call "the new thought of the hour." During his years in Boston, Garland was especially close to the intellectual, somewhat bohemian group surrounding the *Arena*, a society whose interests ranged from evolutionary theory to women's dress reform and psychic investigation. Many of the issues raised in *Crumbling Idols* were undoubtedly discussed during the long evenings Garland spent with friends

[2] Jesse Sidney Goldstein, "Two Literary Radicals: Garland and Markham in Chicago," *American Literature*, XVII (May 1945), 158.

[3] Hamlin Garland, *Companions on the Trail* (New York, 1931), p. 461.

like the actors Mr. and Mrs. James A. Herne, in whose home "oft-quoted volumes of Spencer, Darwin, Fiske, Carlyle, Ibsen, Valdes, Howells" gave evidence that they were not only "abreast but ahead of the current thought of the day." [4] In reworking his articles for publication in book form, Garland deleted some conspicuous sops to his liberal editors: a long passage on literary evolution and an explicit statement of Ibsen's social message, as well as a bold-faced commercial for the *Arena*. But Garland did not succeed in removing from *Crumbling Idols* all traces of his earlier connections with the Eastern magazines. In the text itself previous publication is suggested by the puzzling — apparently uncorrected — date, '92, at the end of Chapter VI. Even Garland's title echoes Flower's cataclysmic sense that the age was marked by "the crash of falling creeds and time-honored dogmas," [5] though, as some contemporaries felt, "Crumbling Idols" is unduly bombastic for a book advocating the day's most popular literary form. Above all, the mélange of avant-garde notions recommended in these essays bears the stamp of an urban, Eastern intellectual society, more sophisticated than any Garland could have found in the West.

In fact, *Crumbling Idols* is but one document from a debate on literary form which, for more than a decade, had raged in the pages of American magazines from the journals of comment, like *Harper's* and the *Atlantic*, to religious publications, like the *Chautauquan* and the *Andover Review*. It may seem strange that an apparently

[4] Garland, "Mr. and Mrs. Herne," *Arena*, IV (Oct. 1891), 551.
[5] "Editorial Notes," *Arena*, V (June 1892), 269.

aesthetic issue centering upon the relative merits of the romance and the realistic novel should have attracted such great and varied interest. Yet the real question was more social than literary: was popular literature demoralizing the nation? The debate over realism is important in American intellectual history because it indicates that through the post-Civil War years the national conscience found relief by attributing social and political errors to the influence of romantic writings. In the history of American letters, this investigation of literary form and purpose is noteworthy because it made way for new developments in fictional style. Though Garland did not initiate or conclude the discussion of the moral and aesthetic purpose of literature, he brought to it fresh insight and flamboyant enthusiasm for social action and artistic experiment.

In *Crumbling Idols* we see Garland as an impassioned propagandist but not as a wholly original thinker. Many of the literary notions he recommends in these essays had already been endorsed by leaders of the Eastern literary establishment. William Dean Howells, an Ohioan by birth but an Easterner by long association, expressed similar views in *Criticism and Fiction* (1891), a volume which like *Crumbling Idols* contained much previously published material. A comparison of *Crumbling Idols* with *Criticism and Fiction* and other comment from "The Editor's Study," Howells' column in *Harper's*, suggests there was justice in the contemporary opinion that Garland had been educated and guided by the elder man of letters. Most of the authors and critics Garland cites had been discussed by Howells. He, too, had encouraged local colorists and condemned American imitation of traditional European fictional methods and critical standards. Howells agreed with Valdes that beauty is an expression of "the true meaning of things,"[6] a view which suggests Garland's notion of "veritism." Certainly Howells' exhortation to the contemporary writer —

Do not trouble yourselves about standards or ideals; but try to be faithful and natural; remember that there is no greatness, no beauty, which does not come from truth to your own knowledge of things; and keep on working, even if your work is not long remembered.[7]

— would have made an admirable motto for *Crumbling Idols*.

Could such things be measured, Garland's unacknowledged debt to Howells might prove greater than his avowed debt to Walt Whitman. There is, of course, an echo of Whitman's language in Garland's prose: the catalogues of names, the celebration of colorful scenes in a diverse American landscape. A trace of Whitman's love of health, especially in women, may be discerned in *Crumbling Idols*, but it is more evident in a novel like *Rose of Dutcher's Cooly*. Whitman's speculations on the need for a uniquely American art and an "ethic" quality in American literature, particularly the comments evoked by the trip through the West recorded in *Specimen Days*, must also have pleased Garland. Finally, Whitman's interest in evolutionary thought is memorialized in the motto which

[6] W. D. Howells, *Criticism and Fiction*, ed. Clara and Rudolf Kirk (New York, 1959), p. 34.
[7] *Ibid.*, p. 69.

Garland said he chose from the *Collect*. There is, however, no sign in *Crumbling Idols* of Whitman's major theme: the unifying force of a national literature inspired by "a great composite democratic individual." Indeed, Garland does not even seem to share that faith in the epic function of poetry which James Russell Lowell expressed in the essay quoted in Chapter XI. Like others of his generation, Garland had abandoned both the method and the ideology of earlier American literature. Although he pays homage to Whitman and Lowell, he had effectively disowned the epic vision of these older literary theorists.

The age of Whitman and Lowell was separated from the era of Howells and Garland by civil war. Many of the social and moral problems raised by a great internal struggle are reflected in the critical atmosphere which produced *Crumbling Idols*. The literary nationalism which condemned Sir Walter Scott and his imitators because — as Mark Twain suggested in discussing the South's castles and culture — the romance fostered a feudal frame of mind that led to war is, of course, a way of saying Americans had not fought brothers but pseudo-Europeans. The local color movement was a form of literary nationalism which magnified the sectional differences dramatized by the Civil War, but minimized the element of foreign influence. A "scientific" outlook, whether adapted from Taine, Darwin, or Spencer, seemed consistent with local color and other forms of realism not only because it invited close attention to the facts of natural setting or regional dialect, but also because it invalidated emotional extremes — like Villainy or Perfect Love — so often found in romances and so rarely in American life.[8] Advocates of literary realism contended that the romance was responsible for many of the social ills of America. Both the old feudalism of the defeated South and the new feudalism of the robber barons, "with its truly mediaeval inequality between the classes," reflected the degenerate morality of the romance.[9] Fiction which did not portray men within their real "social and physiological limits" led to "suicidal extremes" of moral judgment [10] — such extremes, indeed, as once seemed to justify internecine war. Emotional, imaginative tales at last destroyed the readers' "power to recognize truth" and undermined their ability "to make independent ethical judgments," thus virtually disqualifying them for democratic citizenship.[11]

The realists' criticism of the romantic frame of mind was personified in their portrait of the unreconstructed Southerner: a hot-headed, effusively courteous adventurer, somewhat too handy with the ladies. In contrast, the realists' hero was represented by Ulysses S. Grant: a humble, practical, unimaginative but resourceful "common" man, who bested the chivalric mountebanks of pseudo-feudalism. If a litera-

[8] In "Herbert Spencer and the Genesis of Hamlin Garland's Critical System," *Tulane Studies in English*, VII (New Orleans, 1958), 153–168, Donald Pizer has argued that Garland found the development of local color compatible with Spencer's doctrine of progression from incoherent homogeneity to coherent heterogeneity.

[9] H. H. Boyesen, "The Great Realists and the Empty Story-Tellers," *Forum*, XVIII (Feb. 1895), 725.

[10] W. D. Howells, Review of H. M. Posnett, *Comparative Literature*, "The Editor's Study," *Harper's Monthly*, LXXIII (July 1886), 319.

[11] William Graham Sumner, "The Scientific Attitude of Mind," *Essays* (New Haven, 1934), I, 53–54. See also Thomas Davidson, "Our Servility in Literature," *Forum*, XI (May 1891), 342–49.

ture whose protagonists were modeled on Grant seemed dull, if devotees of the romance urged that tired American businessmen sought relaxation in reading of splendid bygone times, advocates of realism might assert with Howells that truth alone is beautiful, or with Garland that the "present fact" is "haloed, with significance if not beauty." [12]

The moral earnestness which animated the realistic attack upon romanticism also produced schism, or at least semantic confusion, within the ranks of realism. Novels like Zola's, which depicted moral degeneration in an unfavorable environment, were classified not as "naturalism" but as "realism," or sometimes "French realism." In the effort to single out tales depicting either a more favorable adaptation to a sordid environment or the course of life in a more favorable environment, the term "idealism" was often used. This more cheerful literature, the "other side of realism," seemed to some critics to combine "the sweetness, the amenity of romanticism" with "the earnestness, the truth of realism." [13] To others it was a higher realism which represented the "pathos and glory" of man's nobility,[14] the eternal element in human nature that transcends the facts of life.

In effect this critical discussion made a distinction between the method and the philosophy of "realism," which resembles the familiar distinction between romantic style and philosophical romanticism. Realism in method meant

[12] Garland, "A Dialogue Between Eugene Field and Hamlin Garland," *McClure's Magazine*, I (Aug. 1893), 203.

[13] Gamaliel Bradford, "Idealism in Literature," *Andover Review*, VIII (Nov. 1887), 467.

[14] "Contributors' Club," *Atlantic Monthly*, LX (Oct. 1887), 573.

the accurate description of contemporary life. In this sense, local color stories describing the special qualities of a limited community, dialect stories giving an accurate report of peculiar speech patterns, and urban novels portraying the usual life of city dwellers are all realistic. Philosophical realism depicting man as an animal naturally responding to environmental stress could produce such examples of human degeneration as the Maheu family of *Germinal*. Some American realists dismissed Zola and his imitators as "sensationalists" or even "romanticists," but this argument confuses the issue. In fact, many early American realists simply assumed that evolution implied a moral teleology. If for the purposes of fiction some foreshortening was necessary, if the good triumphed sooner than it might in life, the final pattern of the story was nonetheless true to the greater scheme of things. Such realists, like Garland, were able to resist the effeteness of "art for art," because their reading of reality did not deny beauty or the finer emotions.

The opinions of this school of criticism are to modern readers as strange as its terms. Howells — often today condemned for meliorism — was denounced by H. H. Boyesen for emphasizing "trivialities" and excluding from his work "the nobler qualities of the human soul." [15] Another reviewer had, however, praised *The Rise of Silas Lapham* for its moral clarity, noting that "If we are to have a portraiture of moral baseness, we have a right to ask for some shadows so deep as to leave no doubt of their

[15] H. H. Boyesen, "The Romantic and the Realistic Novel," *The Chautauquan*, IX (Nov. 1888), 97.

meaning. . . ." [16] Ed Howe's *The Story of A Country Town* was labeled a "romance," because it was untrue to "Western life which is the most cheerful and rollicking life in the world" and reflected only "Mr. Howe's disgust for its limitations. . . ." [17] Again, Joseph Kirkland's novel, *The McVeys*, was said to exemplify "not the realism of art, but the realism of nature," because it did not set its portrait of human life "in relation with the universal." [18] These are the very terms Garland employed in his criticism of Stephen Crane's *Maggie*, which, he said, was "only a fragment," because it failed to depict "the families living on the next street, who live lives of heroic purity and hopeless hardship." [19]

Like his criticism, Garland's fiction of this period illustrates his attachment to the gentler school of realism. In "Under the Lion's Paw," a story written to illustrate the need for single-tax reform, the downtrodden farmers are perfect exemplars of heroic purity in an environment of hopeless hardship. Though "bent and cold," they are "cheery." Though nearly driven to murder by economic injustice and the sneering cruelty of a moneylender, the protagonist is saved from wrongdoing by the sight of his innocent baby daughter. As an exponent of "art for truth's sake," [20] Garland might be challenged for insisting that

[16] "Recent American Fiction," *Atlantic Monthly*, LVI (Oct. 1885), 555.

[17] "Contributors' Club," *Atlantic Monthly*, LVI (Nov. 1885), 715.

[18] "Illinois Life in Fiction," *Atlantic Monthly*, LXIII (Feb. 1889), 278.

[19] Garland, "An Ambitious French Novel and a Modest American Story," in "Books of the Day," *Arena*, VIII (1893), xii.

[20] Goldstein, "Two Literary Radicals," p. 157.

men so oppressed are also sensitive and refined. But it could be argued that Garland's fiction, because it attracts the reader's sympathy to society's noble sufferers, is a more effective instrument for reform than the work of writers, like Norris or Dreiser, less committed to a sympathetic view of human nature. Certainly, it is not surprising that Garland condemned later literary "progressives" for reviving "old obscenities and vices and crimes," [21] since they, like the harsher realists of the nineties, did not share his faith in man's moral nature. For Garland it was the responsibility of the novelist to depict not only society's wrongs but also man's finer nature struggling toward an inevitably brighter day.[22]

The idealistic strain in Garland's fiction and criticism helps to explain his reference in *Crumbling Idols* to authors like Joel Chandler Harris or Thomas Nelson Page whose work seems predominately "romantic." By writing dialect and local color stories, both Harris and Page proved themselves realists in method. Yet as an advocate of the "other side of realism" Garland could also feel "wonderment" for the "brave skill" of these Southern romancers who had improved upon reality by weaving an atmosphere of en-

[21] Garland, *Back-Trailers From the Middle Border* (New York, 1928), p. 166.

[22] In "Crane Reports Garland on Howells," *Modern Language Notes*, LXX (Jan. 1955), 37–38, n. 4, Donald Pizer suggests that there was either an error in the report that Garland called Howells' literary theory "idealism" or a mistake in Garland's speech labeling Howells' definition of realism as "idealism." Garland is reported as saying that Howells "believes in the progress of ideals, the relative in art." In the light of the above discussion, I suggest that Garland did call Howells an idealist, and that though the term is not Howells' own, Garland accurately described Howells' position in the realistic debate of the day.

chantment and beauty about their drab, defeated land.[23]

The critical issue of idealistic realism also sheds special light on Garland's notion of literary impressionism. In the book on aesthetics which Garland cited as a major source for *Crumbling Idols*, Eugène Véron argued that the value of impressionistic art is derived from the character of the artist. In the artist's work, it is

the manifestation of the faculties and qualities he possesses which attracts and fascinates us. The more sympathetic power and individuality that these faculties and qualities display, the easier it is for them to obtain our love and admiration. On the other hand, we, for a similar reason, reject and contemn bold and vulgar works that by their shortcomings demonstrate the moral and intellectual mediocrity of their authors, and prove the latter to have mistaken their vocation.

Since impressionistic art records "the more or less accidental impression" produced in the artist by "the sight of the object or event rendered," [24] it, more than any other form of art, reveals the moral nature of the perceiver.

The logical difficulty of the idealistic realist is that he insists upon the depiction of noble human qualities which another observer might not perceive and so could call "unreal." By propounding a theory of literary impressionism, which he called "veritism" and defined as "the truthful statement of an individual impression corrected by reference to the fact," [25] Garland nearly resolved the prob-

[23] Garland, *My Friendly Contemporaries* (New York, 1932), pp. 231–232.

[24] Eugène Véron, *Aesthetics*, trans. W. H. Armstrong (London, 1879), p. 107.

[25] Garland, "Productive Conditions of American Literature," *Forum*, XVII (Aug. 1894), 690.

lem of selecting that which is "real." To the veritist the artist's impression is "real" if it is a truthful depiction of what he has seen. If the artist does not see the better side of life, the vertitist may say this does not prove that finer things do not exist, but only that the artist lacks the capacity to perceive them. It would be unwise to credit Garland's theory with logical rigor: by suggesting that the "impression" should be "corrected by reference to the fact," he reintroduced the problem of selection. Yet, in proposing an alliance between realism and impressionism, Garland offered a means of defending traditional morality within the limits imposed by accurate observation and realistic reporting.

Both the origin and the definition of the term "veritism" are obscure. It may be related to the Italian *verismo* — which describes a literary movement also marked by interest in provincial life, dialect, and local color — but there is no evidence that Garland adapted "veritism" from this European source. Because it was not widely accepted in literary discourse, the term cannot be defined by tracing its usage. "Veritism" occasionally appeared in literary criticism published in the *Arena*, and as B. O. Flower employed the term, it seems to signify "that which is real, or, if ideal, is in perfect alignment with the eternal verities as found in life." [26] This usage again suggests that "veritism" meant realism with spiritual content. Garland's coinage, with its overtones of both "the verities" and "the verifiable," is significant because it underlines his concern

[26] B. O. Flower, "Mask or Mirror. The Vital Difference Between Artificiality and Veritism on the Stage," *Arena*, VIII (Aug. 1893), 304.

with the terminology of realism [27] and his alliance with those who, like Howells, felt that the truthful depiction of American life presented a scene more healthy, fortunate, and moral than other literatures afforded. At bottom, Garland testified, "realism," "veritism," and "Americanism" meant "practically the same thing." [28]

In combination with Garland's nationalism, the proclamation of Western literary independence (stated especially in Chapter X and XI of *Crumbling Idols*) may seem anomalous. Probably several strains of thought combined to produce this outburst of sectional patriotism. The emphasis upon individual response to the immediate environment in both local color and impressionism must, of course, commit the Western artist to native themes. Garland also seems to share an old American faith in the health and morality of rural people, a sentiment which implies that their artistic impressions would have special worth. Then, too, the sudden flowering of literary activity in Chicago which accompanied the opening of the World's Fair in 1893 undoubtedly seemed to justify Garland's belief that the West would soon come into its own as an artistic center.

Garland may have had more personal reasons for urging the worth of Western literature. In the early nineties he was himself a young man from the provinces. His apostrophe to Western art might be dismissed as the characteristic gesture of a provincial author who imagines "rich pastures from which he is temporarily walled out" and

---

[27] Garland, "Productive Conditions," p. 690.
[28] Garland, *Roadside Meetings* (New York, 1930), pp. 252–253.

racks "his brain over cunning plans for breaking in." [29]
Moreover, the local writer had some reason to feel neglected, for, as the critic Hamilton Wright Mabie pointed
out in a study of contemporary American reading habits,
the works of "most of the best names in recent native fiction" — among them Harris, Jewett, Murfree, Wilkins, and
Garland — were not in demand in American libraries.[30]
Certainly, *Crumbling Idols* is in part an appeal for the
greater acceptance of regional letters, but the nature of Garland's plea for provincial writing indicates that he found
realism and financial reward compatible. Garland insists that
local writers who have entered the literary marketplace have
been successful. Though he opposes older styles in letters,
he remarks no difference in taste or values between the
Western and the Eastern (or the rural and the urban)
realist. In fact, Garland's critical agreement with the members of the literary establishment who had accepted local
authors left him no recourse but to attribute any prejudice against provincial letters to sectional animosity.

Finally, Garland's personal tradition in the West was
not antagonistic to the East. He was of native American
farmer stock. His forebears, like many others, had moved
West from New England following the lure of abundant
land and found themselves, in the declining years of the
nineteenth century, relatively less prosperous and com-

[29] "Contributors' Club," *Atlantic Monthly*, LVI (Nov. 1885), 715.
[30] Hamilton W. Mabie, "The Most Popular Novels in America,"
Forum, XVI (Dec. 1893), 516. Mabie suggested that the demand for
books by native authors was often reduced by the previous publication
of these same stories in magazines. Since Mabie was concerned only with
the popularity of books, his study does not wholly invalidate Garland's
contention that local writers were successful.

fortable than city-dwellers and other old settlers who had remained in the East.[31] Garland was proud of his Eastern origins, but discontent that rural Westerners did not share the rich life of long-settled seaboard towns. The physical suffering and lack of cultural opportunity which he observed in the West, and particularly his sympathy for the overworked farm wife, led him to support Henry George's single-tax reform. His desire to equalize the farmer's social, as well as his economic, lot is a continuing theme in Garland's appeals for Western improvement. Speaking as a Georgite he declared that if land were "held for use, and not for sale," farmers "would draw together in groups, and with the closer society would come the higher education, art, music, the drama, and the leisure to enjoy all these." [32]

Both Garland's image of the Georgite millennium and his apotheosis of the West in *Crumbling Idols* envisioned the Middle Border remade along the lines of New England. Far from disowning Eastern attitudes, Garland in these essays even emulates Eastern forms in the method of his argument. Though he criticizes the literary establishment which adopts foreign criteria of taste and judgment, he is careful to validate his literary theory by referring to the similar opinions of distinguished European artists. As an evolutionist Garland seems to argue that the undeveloped West will be the site of a new cultural development inspired by

[31] For a full discussion of the role of social status in agrarian discontent of the nineties, see Richard Hofstadter, *The Age of Reform* (New York, 1956), pp. 23–130.

[32] From a report of Garland's speech in the *Standard*, Nov. 26, 1887, quoted in Donald Pizer, "Hamlin Garland in the *Standard*," *American Literature*, XXVI (Nov. 1954), 404.

the world's most recent thought. Yet the opening contention in Chapter X — "If the West had been settled first,
the East would be a wilderness to-day" and the West
would be "the home of all ease, refinement, culture and
art" — suggests that Garland would not have quarreled
with a *Western* cultural establishment. Neither dislike for
the East nor yet a stringent application of evolutionary
theory is revealed in Garland's sectionalism. It is, more
simply, a protest against the inevitable injustice of a
cultural lag in the provinces.

Garland's prediction that inland artistic centers would
unseat the cultural leadership of the East was not fulfilled.
In the later years of the nineteenth century the provincial
peculiarities recorded by local literature either had vanished, or as Mary E. Wilkins Freeman suggested, belonged
to "a present" that was "rapidly becoming *past*." [33] Even
as Garland wrote, improving means of mass communication were fast erasing the special regional qualities which
justified independent provincial movements in art and letters. Some of the populistic discontent manifested in Garland's appeal for a richer cultural life in the West was alle-
viated by the growth of great inland cities and by economic
policies which insured a fuller life for the American farmer.
But, as Garland was himself to find, the leisurely life devoted to art, music, and drama was not compatible with the
necessities, or perhaps the ambitions, of an American farm-
ing community.

The failure of his ideal of Western development eventu-
ally changed the course of Garland's life. His years in

[33] Garland, *Roadside Meetings*, p. 34.

West Salem, Wisconsin, were marked by pathetic attempts to bring the city's ease and luxuries to a home on the Middle Border. They were marred by his growing loneliness for the cosmopolitan artistic society of the Eastern seaboard. At last Garland decided that if he could not "change the condition" of Western Americans, he would "live away from them." [34] Nearly a quarter of a century after the publication of *Crumbling Idols* he joined the procession of "back-trailers from the Middle Border," because West Salem represented a "narrow bound" for his family and a "sad exile" for him.[35] He never again ventured far from the great centers which are both the marketplace of literature and the meetingplace of artists.

The ideas and hopes expressed in this early volume are not invalidated because they were not memorialized in social change. Naturalism superseded idealism; Sister Carrie, who like Hamlin Garland sought life's "better things," found no escape from discontent in the richer life of the city or even in the "artistic" world of the urban theatre. The disenchantment of this later literature cannot be found in Garland's critical or imaginative work. Just as *Crumbling Idols* — despite its radical tone — reveals his acceptance of the prevailing literary mores and the cultural standards of the nineties, Garland's fictional attempts at social criticism — though they protest transient injustices — attest his fundamental acceptance of American society. Yet for those who have observed the literary procession of "irresponsibles," "expatriates," and a "beat" generation,

---

[34] Garland, *Afternoon Neighbors* (New York, 1934), p. 128.
[35] Garland, *Back-Trailers from the Middle Border*, p. 16.

INTRODUCTION

Crumbling Idols is an important reminder of an age when the youthful American artist did not seek isolation from his society. A young man's book, *Crumbling Idols* is redolent with the vigor, ambition, and idealism of first maturity. It is also illogical, elliptic, emotional, and boyishly unselfconscious. Still it continues to deserve thoughtful attention because it is a challenging attempt to define a form of artistic fulfillment wholly consistent with social responsibility.

Jane Johnson

Cambridge, Massachusetts
August 1959

Scholars have long noted that some or all of the essays in *Crumbling Idols* were published before they were joined together in book form. In 1893 a contemporary, Edwin Markham, believed that most of the essays had not yet been written,[1] and Garland planned to send galley proof of the book to several friends for their opinion — an unnecessary gesture, it would seem, if the material was already in print.[2] The editor has found part or all of eight chapters of *Crumbling Idols* in four articles published by Garland between 1890 and 1893. Of the three chapters remaining, the title of one — "The Drift of the Drama" — appears as the title of a "special lecture" which Garland listed in the *Literary World* in 1896. Although this list postdates *Crumbling Idols* by two years, Garland's lecture material may have been prepared and delivered much earlier.

Chapter IX ("Impressionism") might also have been the core of, or adapted from, another lecture, "Impressionism in Art," which appears on the same list.[3] Because most of the artists mentioned in this chapter exhibited at the Chicago World's Fair, and because Garland cites the Fair's showings specifically, Chapter IX must have been written after Garland went to Chicago in 1893. In *A Daughter of the Middle Border* (pp. 2–3), Garland tells of giving a lecture

---

[1] Jesse Goldstein, "Two Literary Radicals: Garland and Markham in Chicago, 1893," *American Literature*, XVII, 2 (May 1945), 160.

[2] John T. Flanagan, "Hamlin Garland Writes to His Chicago Publisher," *American Literature*, XXIII, 4 (Jan. 1952), 453–454.

[3] *Literary World* (N.Y.), XXVII, 4 (Feb. 22, 1896), 56.

on "Impressionism in Art" at the home of Franklin Head in Chicago. This lecture may well have presented the material of Chapter IX previous to its appearance in *Crumbling Idols*.

The four articles which contributed to eight chapters in *Crumbling Idols* were considerably revised for the book. There are numerous omissions from and additions to the earlier text, as well as extensive changes in such technical matters as paragraphing and punctuation. This is apparently the revision to which Garland referred in writing his editors that he had "knitted the whole thing together and improved it very much." [4] The extent of his revisions also suggests why he sought comment on the book as if it were a new work.

The following list indicates in detail the relation of the earlier articles to the chapters mentioned.

1) From "The West in Literature," *Arena*, VI, 6 (Nov. 1892), 669–676:
Chapter I ("Provincialism"); two paragraphs in Chapter VI ("The Local Novel"), pp. 63–64 in this edition, which appeared on p. 674 in the *Arena* article; and the first five paragraphs of Chapter III ("The Question of Success") which appeared on pp. 674–675 of the *Arena* article, as well as the last paragraph of Chapter III which was also the concluding paragraph of the *Arena* article.

2) From "The Future of Fiction," *Arena*, VII, 5 (April 1893), 513–524:
Chapter IV ("Literary Prophecy") follows the text of the article pp. 513–520; Chapter VI ("The Local Novel") follows the text of the same article, pp. 520–523, except,

---

[4] Flanagan, pp. 453–454.

NOTE ON THE TEXT

of course, for the two paragraphs from the earlier article, "The West in Literature."

3) From "Ibsen as Dramatist," *Arena*, II, 1 (June 1890), 72–82:

Chapter VIII ("The Influence of Ibsen").

4) From "The Literary Emancipation of the West," *The Forum*, XVI, 2 (Oct. 1893), 156–166:

Chapter X ("Literary Centres"), p. 113 through the fourth paragraph on p. 122 of this edition follows the text of the *Forum* article, pp. 156–161 (top); Chapter XI ("Literary Masters"), p. 127 through the first paragraph on p. 134 follows the article, pp. 161–165 (top); three paragraphs in Chapter XII ("Afterword"), p. 142 (bottom) to p. 144 (top) in this edition appeared on pp. 165–166 of the *Forum* article.

Garland's article, "Productive Conditions of American Literature," *Forum*, XVII, 6 (Aug. 1894), 690–698, restates points made in *Crumbling Idols*. There are similar phrases, but no part of the text matches the text of this book.

Hamlin Garland apparently made no attempt to reproduce the longer quotations in *Crumbling Idols* accurately. To simplify the appearance of this edition, the editor has not indicated the points at which punctuation in Garland's quotations differs from that of the published source.

Again to simplify this edition, the writers and artists Garland names are not identified in the textual notes. The less familiar names appear in the Biographical Glossary with a brief statement of information relevant to the citation in *Crumbling Idols*.

CRUMBLING IDOLS

*Twelve Essays on Art
Dealing Chiefly With Literature,
Painting and the Drama*

TO THE MEN AND WOMEN OF AMERICA
WHO HAVE THE COURAGE TO BE ARTISTS

To love the truth in an age of lies;
To hold fast art when hunger cries;
To sing love's song in spite of hate,
Keeping his heart inviolate, —
These are the artist's victories.

A PERSONAL WORD

This book is not a history; it is not a formal essay: it is a series of suggestions.

I do not assume to speak for any one but myself, — being an individualist, — and the power of this writing to destroy or build rests upon its reasonableness, simply. It does not carry with it the weight of any literary hierarchy.

It is intended to weaken the hold of conventionalism upon the youthful artist. It aims also to be constructive, by its statement and insistent re-statement that American art, to be enduring and worthy, must be original and creative, not imitative.

My contention is not against literary artists of the past, but against fetichism. Literary prostration is as hopeless and sterile as prostration before Baal or Isis or Vishnu. It is fitter to stand erect in these days.

Youth should study the past, not to get away from the present, but to understand the present and to anticipate the future. I believe in the mighty pivotal present. I believe in the living, not the dead. The men and women around me interest me more than the saints and heroes of other centuries.

I do not advocate an exchange of masters, but freedom from masters. Life, Nature, — these should be our teachers. They are masters who do not enslave.

Youth should be free from the dominion of the dead; therefore I defend the individual right of the modern creative mind to create in the image of life, and not in the image of any literary master, living or dead.

3

A PERSONAL WORD

There came a young man to Monet, saying, "Master, teach me to paint." To which Monet replied, "I do not teach painting; I make paintings. There never has been, and there never will be, but one teacher: there she is!" and with one sweep of his arm he showed the young man the splendor of meadow and sunlight. "Go, learn of her, and listen to all she will say to you. If she says nothing, enter a notary's office and copy papers; that, at least, is not dishonorable, and is better than copying nymphs."

It is this spirit which is reinvigorating art in every nation of Europe; and shall we sit down and copy the last epics of feudalism, and repeat the dying echoes of Romance?

I

PROVINCIALISM

I. PROVINCIALISM

The history of American literature is the history of provincialism slowly becoming less all-pervasive — the history of the slow development of a distinctive utterance.

By provincialism I mean dependence upon a mother country for models of art production. This is the sense in which Taine or Véron would use the word. The "provincialism" which the conservative deplores is not provincialism, but the beginning of an indigenous literature.

"The true makers of national literature," writes Posnet[t], in his "Comparative Literature," "are the actions and thoughts of the nation itself. The place of these can never be taken by the sympathies of a cultured class too wide to be national, or those of a central academy too refined to be provincial. Provincialism is no ban in a truly national literature." [1]

Using the word "provincialism," therefore, from the point of view of the central academy, we have had too little of it. That is to say, our colonial writers from 1800 on to 1860, had too little to do with the life of the American people, and too much concern with British critics. Using it in its literary sense of dependence upon England and classic models, we have had too much of it. It has kept us timidly imitating the great writers of a nation far separated from us naturally in its social and literary ideals.

The whole development can be epitomized thus: Here

---

[1] Hutcheson Macauley Posnett, *Comparative Literature* (N.Y., 1886), p. 345.

7

on the eastern shore of America lay a chain of colonies predominantly English, soon to be provinces. Like all colonists, they looked back to their mother-country for support and encouragement in intellectual affairs as in material things. They did not presume to think for themselves. But the Revolution taught them something. It strengthened the feeling of separate identity and responsibility. It liberated them in politics, but left them still provincial (dependent) in literary and religious things. There still remained some truth in the British sneer, that American poets and artists were merely shadows or doubles successively of Pope, of Scott, of Byron, of Wordsworth, and of Tennyson. In all the space between the Revolution and the Civil War, American poets reflected the American taste fairly well, but the spirit and form of their work (with a few notable exceptions) was imitative.

Here and there song was sung, from the sincere wish to embody American life and characteristic American thought. Each generation grew less timid, and more manly and individual. The Civil War came on, and was an immense factor in building up freedom from old-world models, and in developing native literature. National feeling had an immense widening and deepening. From the interior of America, men and women rose almost at once to make American literature take on vitality and character.

American life had been lived, but not embodied in art. Native utterance had been overawed and silenced by academic English judgments; but this began to change after the Civil War. The new field began to make itself felt, not all at once, but by degrees, through "Snow-bound" and "The Biglow Papers"[2] and "The Tales of the Argonauts"[3] and the "Songs of the Sierras."[4] But while this change was growing, there was coming in in the Eastern cities the spirit of a central academy that was to stand in precisely the same relation to the interior of America that London formerly occupied with regard to the whole country.

It may be that New York is to threaten and overawe the interior of America, as Paris reigns over the French provinces. The work of Mistral and the *Felibrige* may be needed with us to keep original genius from being silenced or distorted by a central academy which is based upon tradition rather than upon life and nature. Decentralization may come to be needed here, as in Europe.

The evolutionist explains the past by the study of laws operative in the present, and by survivals of ancient conditions obscurely placed in modern things, like sinking icebergs in a southern sea. The attitude of mind (once universal with Americans) which measured everything by British standards, and timidly put new wine into old bottles, can still be found among the academic devotees and their disciples. They are survivals of a conception of life and literature once universal.

The change which has taken place can be specifically illustrated in the West. That is to say, the general terms which could be applied to the whole country up to the

[2] Garland errs in implying that James Russell Lowell's *Biglow Papers*, of which the first series appeared in 1848, belongs to the post-Civil War period.

[3] The first of Bret Harte's collections to bear this title is *Tales of the Argonauts and Other Sketches* (1875).

[4] By Joaquin Miller; published 1871.

time of the Civil War can be applied specifically to the middle West to-day. As a Western man, I think I may speak freely, without being charged with undue prejudice toward the States I name.

The school-bred West, broadly speaking, is as provincial in its art as it is assertive of Americanism in politics. The books it reads, the pictures it buys, are nearly all of the conventional sort, or worse yet, imitations of the conventional. Its literary clubs valiantly discuss dead issues in English literature, and vote in majority against the indigenous and the democratic. They have much to say of the ideal and the universal in literature, quite in the manner of their academical instructors.

The lower ranks of Western readers, as everywhere, devour some millions of tons of romantic love-stories, or stories of detectives or Indians. It is a curious thing to contrast the bold assertion of the political exhorter of "America for Americans" with the enslavement of our readers and writers to various shades of imitative forms of feudalistic literature. America is not yet democratic in art, whatever it may claim to be in politics.

These facts are not to be quarrelled about, they are to be studied. They are signs of life, and not of death. It is better that these people should read such things than nothing at all. They will rise out of it. They can be influenced, but they must be approached on the side of life, and not by way of the academic. They are ready to support and be helped by the art which springs from life.

It is the great intelligent middle class of America, curiously enough, who are apparently most provincial. With them the verdict of the world is all-important. Their education has been just sufficient to make them distrustful of their own judgment. They are largely the product of our schools. They have been taught to believe that Shakespeare ended the drama, that Scott has closed the novel, that the English language is the greatest in the world, and that all other literatures are curious, but not at all to be ranked in power and humanity with the English literature, etc., etc.

I speak advisedly of these things, because I have been through this instruction, which is well-nigh universal. This class is the largest class in America, and makes up the great body of school-bred Westerners. They sustain with a sort of desperation all the tenets of the conservative and romantic criticism in which they have been instructed.

It can almost be stated as a rule without an exception that in our colleges there is no chair of English literature which is not dominated by conservative criticism, and where sneering allusion to modern writers is not daily made. The pupil is taught to worship the past, and is kept blind to the mighty literary movements of his own time. If he comes to understand Ibsen, Tolstoy, Björnson, Howells, Whitman, he must do it outside his instruction.

This instruction is well meaning, but it is benumbing to the faculties. It is essentially hopeless. It blinds the eyes of youth to the power and beauty of the life and literature around him. It worships the past, despises the present, and fears the future. Such teaching is profoundly pessimistic, because it sees literary ideals changing. It has not yet seen that metamorphosis is the law of all living things. It has not yet risen to the perception that the question for America to settle is not whether it can produce something *greater* than the past, but whether it shall produce something *different* from the past. Our task is not to imitate, but to create.

Instruction of this kind inevitably deflects the natural bent of the young artist, or discourages attempt altogether. It is the opposite of education; that is, it represses rather than *leads out* the distinctive individuality of the student.

These conservative ideas affect the local newspapers, and their literary columns are too often full of the same gloomy comment. They are timidly negative when not partisanly conservative. They can safely praise Ruskin and Carlyle, and repeat an old slur on Browning or Whitman.

There is also a class of critics who can launch into two-column criticisms of a new edition of "Rasselas," and leave unread a great novel by Tolstoy, or a new translation of Brand,[5] or a new novel by Howells. Their judgment is worthless to detect truth and beauty in a work of art close at hand. They wait for the judgment of the East, of London.

The American youth is continually called upon by such critics to take Addison or Scott or Dickens or Shakespeare as a model. Such instruction leads naturally to the creation of blank-verse tragedies on Columbus and Washington, — a species of work which seems to the radical the crowning absurdity of misplaced effort.

Thus, the American youth is everywhere turned away from the very material which he could best handle, which

[5] Garland probably means Georg Morris Cohen Brandes (1842–1927), Danish literary critic who encouraged Björnson and Ibsen.

he knows most about, and which he really loves most, — material which would make him individual, and fill him with hope and energy. The Western poet and novelist is not taught to see the beauty and significance of life near at hand. He is rather blinded to it by his instruction.

He turns away from the marvellous changes which border-life subtends in its mighty rush toward civilization. He does not see the wealth of material which lies at his hand, in the mixture of races going on with inconceivable celerity everywhere in America, but with especial pictur-esqueness in the West. If he sees it, he has not the courage to write of it.

If, here and there, one has reached some such perception, he voices it timidly, with an apologetic look in his eye.

The whole matter appears to me to be a question of the individuality. I feel that Véron has stated this truth better than any other man. In his assault upon the central acad-emy he says, in substance, "Education should not con-ventionalize, should not mass together; it should individ-ualize." [6]

The Western youth, like the average school-bred Amer-ican, lacks the courage of his real conviction. He really prefers the modern writer, the modern painter, but he feels bound to falsify in regard to his real mind. As a creative intelligence, he lacks the courage to honestly investigate his surroundings, and then stand by his judgment. Both as reader and writer, he dreads the Eastern comment. It is pitiful to see his eagerness to conform; he will even go beyond his teachers in conforming. Thus he starts wrong.

[6] See Eugène Véron, *L'Esthétique* (Paris, 1878), pp. 153–162.

His standards of comparison are wrong. He is forced into writing to please somebody else, which is fatal to high art.

To perceive the force of all this, and the real hopelessness of instruction according to conventional models, we have only to observe how little that is distinctive has been produced by the great Western middle States, — say Wisconsin, Illinois, and Iowa. Of what does its writing consist?

A multitude of little newspapers, first of all, full of local news; and larger newspapers that are political organs, with some little attention to literature on their inside pages. Their judgments are mainly conservative, but here and there in their news columns one finds sketches of life so vivid one wonders why writers so true and imaginative are not recognized and encouraged.

The most of the short stories in these papers, however, are absolutely colorless, where they are not pirated exotics. In all that they call "literature" these papers generally reflect what they believe to be the correct thing in literary judgment. In their unconscious moments they are fine and true.

Art, they think, is something far away, and literary subjects must be something select and very civilized. And yet for forty years an infinite drama has been going on in those wide spaces of the West, — a drama that is as thrilling, as full of heart and hope and battle, as any that ever surrounded any man; a life that was unlike any ever seen on the earth, and which should have produced its characteristic literature, its native art chronicle.

As for myself, I am overwhelmed by the majesty, the immensity, the infinite charm of the life that goes on

around me. Themes are crying out to be written. Take,
for a single example, the history of the lumbering district
of the northern lakes, — a picturesque and peculiar life,
that through a period of thirty years has been continually
changing in all but a few of its essential features; and yet
this life has had only superficial representation in the
sketches of the tourist or reporter; its inner heart has not
been uttered.

The subtle changes of thought and of life that have
come with the rise of a city like St. Paul or Minneapolis;
the life of the great saw-mills and shingle-mills; and the
river-life of the upper Mississippi are all fine subjects. So
are the river towns like Dubuque and Davenport, with
their survivals of French life reaching down to the present
year, and thus far unrecorded.

Then there is the mixture of races; the coming in of
the German, the Scandinavian; the marked yet subtle
changes in their character. Then there is the building of
railroads, with all their trickery and false promises and
worthless bonds; the rise of millionnaires; the deepening
of social contrasts. In short, there is a great heterogeneous,
shifting, brave population, a land teeming with unrecorded
and infinite drama.

It is only to the superficial observer that this country
seems colorless and dull; to the veritist it is full of burning
interest, greatest possibilities. I instance these localities because I know something special about them; but the same
words apply to Pennsylvania, Ohio, or Kentucky. And
yet how few writers of national reputation this eventful
century-long march of civilization has produced!

We have had the figures, the dates, the bare history, the dime-novel statement of pioneer life, but how few real novels! How few accurate studies of speech and life! There it lies, ready to be put into the novel and the drama, and upon canvas; and it must be done by those born into it. Joaquin Miller has given us lines of splendid poetry touching this life, and Edward Eggleston, Joseph Kirkland, Opie Read, Octave Thanet, have dealt more or less faithfully with certain phases of it; but mainly the mighty West, with its swarming millions, remains undelineated in the novel, the drama, and the poem.

The causes of it, as I have indicated, are twofold: first, lack of a market; and, second, lack of perception. This lack of perception of the art-possibilities of common American life has been due to several causes. Hard life, toil, lack of leisure, have deadened and calloused the perceiving mind, making life hard, dull, and uninteresting. But, beyond this, the right perception has been lacking on the part of instructors and critics. Everything has really tended to repress or distort the art-feeling of the young man or woman. They have been taught to imitate, not to create.

But at last conditions are changing. All over the West young people are coming on who see that every literature in the past was at its best creative and not imitative. Here and there a paper or magazine lends itself to the work of encouraging the young writer in original work. They are likely to err now on the side of flattery. Criticism should be helpful, not indiscriminate either in praise or blame.

And more than this, in every town of the interior there are groups of people whose firmness of conviction and broad culture make them the controlling power in all local literary work. They are reading the most modern literature, and their judgments are not dependent upon New York or London, though they find themselves in full harmony with progressive artists everywhere. They are clearly in the minority, but they are a growing company everywhere, and their influence is felt by every writer of the progressive group.

II

NEW FIELDS

II. NEW FIELDS

The secret of every lasting success in art or literature lies, I believe, in a powerful, sincere, emotional concept of life first, and, second, in the acquired power to convey that concept to others. This leads necessarily to individuality in authorship, and to freedom from past models.

This *theory* of the veritist is, after all, a statement of his passion for truth and for individual expression. The passion does not spring from theory; the theory rises from the love of the verities, which seems to increase day by day all over the Western world.

The veritist, therefore, must not be taken to be dogmatic, only so far as he is personally concerned. He is occupied in stating his sincere convictions, believing that only in that way is the cause of truth advanced. He addresses himself to the mind prepared to listen. He destroys by displacement, not by attacking directly.

It is a settled conviction with me that each locality must produce its own literary record, each special phase of life utter its own voice. There is no other way for a true local expression to embody itself. The sun of truth strikes each part of the earth at a little different angle; it is this angle which gives life and infinite variety to literature. It is the subtle differences which life presents in California and Oregon, for example, which will produce, and justify, a Pacific-Coast literature.

In all that I have written upon local literature, I have told the truth as I saw it. That others did not see it in the same light, was to be expected. And in writing upon Pacific-Coast literature, undoubtedly I shall once more be stating the cause of veritism; for the question of Pacific-Coast literature is really the question of genuine American literature. The same principles apply to all sections of the land.

The mere fact that a writer happens to live in California or Oregon will not make him a part of that literature, any more than Stevenson's life in Samoa will make him a Samoan author. A nation, in the early part of its literary history, is likely to sweep together all that can, by any construction, be called its literature; but as it grows rich in real utterances, it eliminates one after the other all those writings which its clearer judgment perceives to be exotics.

The Pacific Coast is almost like another world. Its distance from New York and Boston, its semi-tropic plants, its strange occupations, place it in a section by itself, just as the rest of the nation falls naturally into New England, the South, the Middle States, and the Northwest; and, in the same way, from the Pacific States will continue to come a distinct local literature. Its vitality depends, in my judgment, upon this difference in quality.

I say "continue to come," because we can never overlook the great work done by Joaquin Miller and Bret Harte. They came to this strange new land, young and impressionable. They became filled with the life and landscape almost with the same power and sincerity as if they had been born here. Miller, especially, at his best, got far below superficial wonder. He attained the love for his subjects which is essential to sincere art. The best of his work could not have been produced anywhere else. It is native as Shasta.

But neither of these men must be taken for model. Veritism, as I understand it, puts aside all models, even living writers. Whatever he may do unconsciously, the artist must consciously stand alone before nature and before life. Nature and life have changed since Miller and Harte wrote. The California of to-day is quite different. The creative writer to-day, if true to himself, finds himself interested in other subjects, and finds himself believing in a different treatment of even the same material.

There is no necessity of treating the same material, however. Vast changes, already in progress, invite the writer. The coming in of horticulture, the immigration of farmers from all the Eastern States; the mingling of races; the feudalistic ownership of lands; the nomadic life of the farmhands, the growth of cities, the passing Spanish civilization, — these are a few of the subjects which occur to me as worthy [of] the best work of novelist and dramatist.

Being "a farmer by birth and a novelist by occupation," I saw most clearly the literary possibilities of the farmer's life in the valleys of California and in the stupendous forests of Oregon.

I saw children moving along to school in the shadow of the most splendid mountains; I saw a youth plowing, — behind him rose a row of palms, against which he stood like a figure of bronze in relief; I saw young men and maidens walking down aisles of green and crimson pepper-trees, and the aisles led to blue silhouetted mountains; I saw men herding cattle where the sun beat with hot radiance, and strange cacti held out wild arms; I saw children playing about cabins, setting at defiance the illimitable width and sunless depths of the Oregon forests, — and I thought, "Perhaps one of these is the novelist or painter of the future."

Perhaps the future poet of these spaces is plowing somewhere like that, because it must be that from the splendor and dramatic contrast of such scenes the poet will rise. He always has, and he always will. His feet will be on the soil like Whittier's, and like Miller's; his song will differ from theirs because he will be an individual soul, and because his time and his environment will not be the same.

Why should the Western artists and poets look away to Greece and Rome and Persia for themes? I have met Western people who were writing blank-verse tragedies of the Middle Ages and painting pictures of sirens and cherubs, and still considered themselves Western writers and Western artists! The reason is not hard to find. They had not risen to the perception of the significant and beautiful in their own environment, or they were looking for effects, without regard to their sincere conviction. They were poets of books, not of life.

This insincerity is fatal to any great work of art. A man must be moved by something higher than money, by something higher than hope of praise; he must have a sleepless love in his heart urging him to re-create in the image the life he has loved. He must be burdened and without rest until he has given birth to his conception. He will not be questioned when he comes; he will be known as a product of some one time and place, a voice speaking the love of his heart.

There was much of dross and effectism in Miller's earlier work, but it was filled with an abounding love of Sierra mountains and forests and moving things, which made him the great figure of the Coast. But the literature which is to come from the Pacific slope, in my judgment, will be intimate and human beyond any California precedent. It will not dodge or equivocate. It will state the truth. It will not be spectacular, it will not deal with the outside (as a tourist must do). It will deal with the people and their home dramas, their loves and their ambitions. It will not seek themes. Themes will crowd upon them and move them.

The lovers who wander down the aisles of orange or lemon or pepper trees will not marvel at blooms and shrubs. Their presence and perfume will be familiar and lovely, not strange. The stark lines of the fir and the broadsword-thrust of the banana-leaf will not attract their surprised look. All will be as friendly and grateful as the maple or the Lombardy poplar to the Iowa school-boy.

A new literature will come with the generation just coming to manhood and womanhood on the Coast. If rightly educated, their eyes will turn naturally to the wheat-fields, the forests, the lanes of orange-trees, the ranges of unsurpassed mountains. They will try to express in the novel, the drama, in painting and in song, the love and interest they take in the things close at hand.

This literature will not deal with crime and abnormities, nor with deceased persons. It will deal, I believe, with the wholesome love of honest men for honest women, with the heroism of labor, the comradeship of men, — a drama of average types of character, infinitely varied, but always characteristic.

In this literature will be the shadow of mountain-islands,

the sweep of dun plains, and dark-blue mountain-ranges silhouetted against a burning yellow sky. It will deal with mighty forests and with man's brave war against the gloom and silence. It will have in it types of vanishing races, and prophecies of coming citizens. It will have the perfume of the orange and lemon trees, the purple dapple of spicy pepper-tree fruit, the grace of drooping, fern-like acacia leaves.

And in the midst of these sights and sounds, moving to and fro in the shadow of these mountains, and feeling the presence of this sea, will be men and women working out the drama of life in a new way, thinking new thoughts, building a happier, sunnier order of things, perhaps, where the laborer will face the winter always without fear and without despondency.

When the real Pacific literature comes, it will not be subject to misunderstanding. It will be such a literature as no other locality could produce, a literature that could not have been written in any other time, or among other surroundings. That is the test of a national literature.

III

THE QUESTION OF SUCCESS

III. THE QUESTION OF SUCCESS

But the question forced on the young writer, even when he is well disposed toward dealing with indigenous material, is, Will it pay? Is there a market for me?

Let me answer by pointing out that almost every novelist who has risen distinctively out of the mass of story-writers in America, represents some special local life or some special social phase.

Mr. Cable stands for the Creole South; Miss Murfree speaks for the mountaineer-life in Tennessee; Joel Harris represents the new study of the negro; Miss Wilkins voices the thought of certain old New England towns; Mr. Howells represents truthful treatment of the cities of Boston and New York; Joseph Kirkland has dealt with early Illinois life; Harold Frederic has written two powerful stories of interior New York life; and so on through a list of equally brave and equally fine writers.

I think it may be said, therefore, that success in indigenous lines is every year becoming more certain. You will not find your market in the West yet, but the great magazines of the country are every year gaining in Americanism.

If we look away to England, we see the same principle illustrated. The most vital blood of the English novel to-day comes from the Provinces. Barrie with his "A Window in Thrums," Kipling with his "Tales of the Hills," Olive Schreiner with "An African Farm," Jane Barlow with "Irish Idyls," are putting to rout the two-volume British novel, which never leaves anything out or puts anything in. It is precisely the same movement which is going on in Norway, Holland, Hungary, — all over Europe, in fact. Wherever the common man rises to the power of stating his interest in life, it takes the form of local fiction.

The consideration of success, however, is not the power which makes the true artist. Deeper yet must be the keen creative delight, — the sweetest, deepest pleasure the artist knows; the passion which sends him supperless to bed in order that his story shall reflect his own ideal, his own concept of life.

But it may be concluded that the encouragement of this local fiction will rob our literature of its dignity. There is no dignity in imitation, it is mere pretence; to seek dignity in form is like putting on stilts. The assumption of the epic by an American poet is like putting a chimney-pot hat on a child. If we insist on sincerity, the question of dignity will take care of itself. Truth is a fine preparation for dignity, and for beauty as well.

Art, I must insist, is an individual thing, — the question of one man facing certain facts and telling his individual relations to them. His first care must be to present his own concept. This is, I believe, the essence of veritism: "Write of those things of which you know most, and for which you care most. By so doing you will be true to yourself, true to your locality, and true to your time."

I am a Western man; my hopes and ambitions for the West arise from absolute knowledge of its possibilities. I want to see its prairies, its river banks and coules, its matchless skies, put upon canvas. I want to see its young writers writing better books, its young artists painting pictures that are true to the life they live and the life they know. I want to see the West supporting its own painters and musicians and novelists; and to that end I want to state my earnest belief, which I have carefully matched with the facts of literary history, that, to take a place in the long line of poets and artists in the English language, the Western writer must, above all other things, be true to himself and to his time. To imitate is fatal. *Provincialism (that is to say, localism) is no ban to a national literature.*

IV

LITERARY PROPHECY

IV. LITERARY PROPHECY

It is interesting to observe that all literary movements in the past had little or no prevision. The question of their future, their permanence, did not disturb them. My reading does not disclose to me that Euphues or Spenser ever thought of the dark future. Each school lived for its day and time, apparently, without disturbing prophecy.

Pope, the monarch of the circumscribed, the emperor of literary lace and ruffles, so far as I have read, had no gloomy forebodings. His dictatorship was the most absolutely despotic and long-continued dictatorship the literary history of England has ever seen. He could be pardoned for never imagining that real flowers could come to be enjoyed better than gilt and scarlet paper roses, all alike. It is not to be wondered at that he had no prevision of Whitman or Ibsen, in the joyous jog-trot of his couplets.

It is probable that where any thought of the future troubled the artist, it unnerved him. Thomas Browne saw oblivion like a dark sea beneath him, but his view of life was mainly statical; he had no basis for optimistic outlook. His skies were hung with black.

Take larger movements, — the Reformation, for example. This movement, in its day, filled the whole religious history of Europe. It transformed empires, and planted colonies in the wilderness of the west. It dominated art, literature, architecture, laws, and yet it was but a phase of intellectual development. Its order was transitory; and had an evolutionist been born into that austere time, he would have predicted the reaction to enjoyment of worldly things which followed, and would have foretold the sure passing away of the whole world as it was then colored and dominated by puritanic thought.

In art, this narrowness and sincerity of faith in itself has been the principal source of power of every movement in the past. To question was to weaken. Had Spenser suspected the prosiness and hollow absurdity of his combats (wherein the hero always wins), had he perceived something else in life better worth while than allegory and the endless recounting of tales of chivalry, he would have failed to embody as he did the glittering and caparisoned barbarism of his forbears. And the crown which Pope wore would have rested like a plat of thorns on his brow had he been visited by disturbing visions of a time when men would prefer their poetry in some other form than couplets or quatrains, and would even question whether the "Essay on Man" was poetry or not.

With no conception of what the world had been, they had no guiding line to point to that which the world was to be. The statical idea of life and literature held in all thought, — except where men believed the world was fallen from a golden age into darkness and decay, or that it was again declining to a fall.

Because Shakespeare and the group around him were feudalistic, and did not believe in the common personality; because the critics of Dryden's day believed Shakespeare was a savage; because each age believed in its art and in the world of thought around it, — therefore has each real age of literature embodied more or less faithfully its own outlook upon life, and gone peacefully, if not arrogantly, to its grave at last, in blessed ignorance of the green dust which the library of the future held in store for it.

In the thought of philosophers, so-called, the same traditional feeling held. The observer, the independent investigator of facts, could hardly be said to have existed. Tradition, the organized conceptions of the race, reigned over the individual, and men did not think. The Scriptures had said it all. There was no room for science.

But while each age can be held in general terms to have had no prevision, it is probable that some few of its greatest minds caught a glimpse of coming change, and that this power of prophecy grew slowly, and the power of tradition grew less binding, until there came upon the world the splendid light of the development theory, uttered by Spencer and Darwin. I think it is not too much to say that, previous to the writing of these men, definite prevision, even on the broadest lines, was impossible, either in sociology or literature.

Until men came to see system and progression, and endless but definite succession in art and literature as in geologic change; until the law of progress was enunciated, no conception of the future and no reasonable history of the past could be formulated. Once prove literature and art subject to social conditions, to environment and social conformation, and the dominance of the epic in one age, and of the drama in another, became as easy to understand and to infer as any other fact of a people's history.

The study of evolution has made the present the most critical and self-analytical of all ages known to us. It has liberated the thought of the individual as never before, and the power of tradition grows fainter year by year.

It is not my purpose to write the history of the development of literature. I have drifted farther into the general subject than I intended. I am merely preparing the way for some more or less valuable ideas upon the future of American fiction.

Evolutionists explain the past by means of laws operative in the present, by survivals of change. In an analogous way, we may infer (broadly, of course) the future of society, and therefore its art, from changes just beginning to manifest themselves. The developed future is always prophesied in the struggling embryos of the present. In the mold of the present are the swelling acorns of future forests.

Fiction already commands the present in the form of the novel of life. It already outranks verse and the drama as a medium of expression. It is so flexible, admits of so many points of view, and comprehends so much (uniting painting and rhythm to the drama and the pure narrative), that it has come to be the highest form of expression in Russia, Germany, Norway, and France. It occupies with easy tolerance the high seats in the synagogue, and felicitates the other arts on having got in, — or rather stayed in at all. At its best it certainly is the most modern and unconventional of arts.

Taking it as it stands to-day in America, the novel not only shows its relation to the past and the present, but it holds within itself prophecies of impending change. No other medium of art expression is so sensitive to demand. Change is sure. What will it be?

We are about to enter the dark. We need a light. This flaming thought from Whitman will do for the search-light of the profound deeps: All that the past was not, the future will be.

If the past was bond, the future will be free. If the past was feudalistic, the future will be democratic. If the past ignored and trampled upon women, the future will place them side by side with men. If the child of the past was ignored, the future will cherish him. And fiction will embody these facts.

If the past was dark and battleful and bloody and barbarous, the future will be peaceful and sunny. If the past celebrated lust and greed and love of power, the future will celebrate continence and humility and altruism. If the past was the history of a few titled personalities riding high on obscure waves of nameless, suffering humanity, the future will be the day of high average personality, the abolition of all privilege, the peaceful walking together of brethren, equals before nature and before the law. And fiction will celebrate this life.

If the past was gross and materialistic in its religion, worshipping idols of wood and stone, demanding sacrifices to appease God, using creed as a club to make men conform to a single interpretation of man's relation to nature and his fellows, then the future will be high and pure and subtle in its religious interpretations; and there will be granted to individuals perfect freedom in the interpretation of nature's laws, a freedom in fact, as well as in name. And to fiction is given the task of subtilely embodying this splendid creed.

All that the past was not, the future will be. The question is not one of similarity, but of difference.

As we run swiftly over the development of literary history, we see certain elements being left behind while others are carried forward. Those which are carried forward are, however, extremely general and fundamental. They are the bones of art, not its curve of flesh or flush of blood.

One of these central elements of unchanging power, always manifest in every really great literature, is sincerity in method. This produces contemporaneousness. The great writers of the past did not write "for all time,"—not even for the future. They mainly were occupied in interesting some portion of their fellow-men. Shakespeare had no care and little thought of the eighteenth century in his writing.

He studied his time, and tried sincerely to state it in terms that would please those whom he considered his judicious friends. Thus he reflected (indirectly) the feudal age, for that was the dominant thought of his day. So Dryden and Pope, each at his best, portrayed his day, putting his sincere and original comment upon the life around him, flavoring every translation he made with the vice and lawlessness which he felt to be the prevailing elements of his immediate surroundings. In the main, they believed in themselves.

Measured by our standard, the writers of the Restoration period were artificial in manner and vile in thought. They smell always of the bawdy-house, and their dramas sicken us with the odor of the filth through which their writers reeled the night before. To themselves they were elegant, truthful, and worthy of being taken seriously at their best and forgiven for their worst.

The romantic school of fiction, while it reigned, was self-justifiable, at least in great figures like Scott and Hugo, because it was a sincere expression of their likings and dislikings. It reflected directly and indirectly their rebellion against the old, and put in evidence their conception of the office of literature. It was also wholesome, and, in Hugo, consciously humanitarian. The romancers did their work. It will never be done so well again, because all that follows their model will be imitative; theirs was the genuine romanticism.

The fiction of the future will not be romantic in any such sense as Scott or Hugo was romantic, because to do that would be to re-live the past, which is impossible; to imitate models, which is fatal. Reader and writer will both be wanting. The element of originality follows from the power of the element of sincerity. "All original art," says Taine, "is self-regulative." [1] It does not imitate. It does not follow models. It stands before life, and is accountant to life and self only. Therefore, the fiction of the future must be original, and therefore self-regulative.

The fiction of the past dealt largely with types, often with abstractions or caricatures. It studied men in heroic attitudes. It concerned itself mainly with love and war. It did not study men intimately, except in vicious or criminal moods.

As fiction has come to deal more and more with men and

[1] Cf. H. A. Taine, *Histoire de la Littérature Anglaise* (Paris, 1863–1864), I, xlii–xlviii.

less with abstractions, it will be safe to infer that this will continue. Eugène Véron covered the ground fully when he said, "We care no longer for gods or heroes; we care for men." [2] This is true of veritism, whose power and influence augment daily; even the romance writers feel its influence, and are abandoning their swiftly running love-stories for studies of character. Like the romantic school of painting, they are affected by the influence they fear.

The novels of Bulwer, Scott, and Hugo, are, after all, mixed with aristocratic influence, though Hugo had much more of what might be called the modern spirit, even in his so-called historical studies.

It is safe to say that the fiction of the future will grow more democratic in outlook and more individualistic in method. Impressionism, in its deeper sense, means the statement of one's own individual perception of life and nature, guided by devotion to truth. Second to this great principle is the law that each impression must be worked out faithfully on separate canvases, each work of art complete in itself. Literalism, the book that can be quoted in bits, is like a picture that can be cut into pieces. It lacks unity. The higher art would seem to be the art that perceives and states the relations of things, giving atmosphere and relative values as they appeal to the sight.

Because the novels of the past were long, involved, given to discussion and comment upon the action, so the novel of the future will be shorter and simpler and less obvious in its method. It will put its lessons into general effect rather than into epigrams. Discussion will be in the relations of its

[2] Eugène Véron, *L'Esthétique,* p. 410.

characters, not on quotable lines or paragraphs. Like impressionism in painting, it will subordinate parts to the whole.

It will teach, as all earnest literature has done, by effect; but it will not be by direct expression, but by placing before the reader the facts of life as they stand related to the artist. This relation will not be put into explanatory notes, but will address itself to the perception of the reader.

Turning our attention for a moment to the actualities of modern fiction, we find destructive criticism to be the most characteristic literary expression of the present and of the immediate future, because of this slow rising of the literary mind to prevision of change in life.

Because the fictionist of to-day sees a more beautiful and peaceful future social life, and, in consequence, a more beautiful and peaceful literary life, therefore he is encouraged to deal truthfully and at close grapple with the facts of his immediate present. His comment virtually amounts to satire or prophecy, or both. Because he is sustained by love and faith in the future, he can be mercilessly true. He strikes at thistles, because he knows the unrotted seed of loveliness and peace needs but sun and the air of freedom to rise to flower and fragrance.

The realist or veritist is really an optimist, a dreamer. He sees life in terms of what it might be, as well as in terms of what it is; but he writes of what is, and, at his best, suggests what is to be, by contrast. He aims to be perfectly truthful in his delineation of his relation to life, but there is a tone, a color, which comes unconsciously into his utterance, like the sobbing stir of the muted violins beneath the frank, clear song of the clarionet; and this tone is one of sorrow that the good time moves so slowly in its approach.

He aims to hasten the age of beauty and peace by delineating the ugliness and warfare of the present; but ever the converse of his picture rises in the mind of the reader. He sighs for a lovelier life. He is tired of warfare and diseased sexualism, and Poverty, the mother of Envy. He is haggard with sympathetic hunger, and weary with the struggle to maintain his standing place on this planet, which he conceives was given to all as the abode of peace. With this hate in his heart and this ideal in his brain the modern man writes his stories of life. They are not always pleasant, but they are generally true, and always they provoke thought.

This element of sad severity will change as conditions change for the common man, but the larger element of sincerity, with resulting contemporaneousness, will remain. Fiction, to be important and successful, must be original and suited to its time. As the times change, fiction will change. This must always be remembered.

The surest way to write for all time is to embody the present in the finest form with the highest sincerity and with the frankest truthfulness. The surest way to write for other lands is to be true to our own land and true to the scenes and people we love, and love in a human and direct way without being educated up to it or down to it.

The people can never be educated to love the past, to love Shakespeare and Homer. Students may be taught to believe they believe, but the great masses of American readers want the modern comment. They want the past colored to suit their ideas of life, — that is, the readers of romance; on higher planes of reading they want sincere delineation of modern life and thought, and Shakespeare, Wordsworth, Dante, Milton, are fading away into mere names, — books we should read but seldom do.

Thus it will be seen that the fiction of the immediate future will be the working out of plans already in hand. There is small prophecy in it, after all. We have but to examine the ground closely, and we see the green shoots of the coming harvest beneath our very feet. We have but to examine closely the most naïve and local of our novels, and the coming literature will be foreshadowed there. The local novelist seems to be the coming woman! Local color is the royal robe.

V

LOCAL COLOR IN ART

V. LOCAL COLOR IN ART

Local color in fiction is demonstrably the life of fiction. It is the native element, the differentiating element. It corresponds to the endless and vital charm of individual peculiarity. It is the differences which interest us; the similarities do not please, do not forever stimulate and feed as do the differences. Literature would die of dry rot if it chronicled the similarities only, or even largely.

Historically, the local color of a poet or dramatist is of the greatest value. The charm of Horace is the side light he throws on the manners and customs of his time. The vital in Homer lies, after all, in his local color, not in his abstractions. Because the sagas of the North delineate more exactly how men and women lived and wrought in those days, therefore they have always appealed to me with infinitely greater power than Homer.

Similarly, it is the local color of Chaucer that interests us to-day. We yawn over his tales of chivalry which were in the manner of his contemporaries, but the Miller and the Priest interest us. Wherever the man of the past in literature showed us what he really lived and loved, he moves us. We understand him, and we really feel an interest in him.

Historically, local color has gained in beauty and suggestiveness and humanity from Chaucer down to the present day. Each age has embodied more and more of its actual life and social conformation until the differentiating qualities of modern art make the best paintings of Norway as distinct in local color as its fiction is vital and indigenous.

Every great moving literature to-day is full of local color. It is this element which puts the Norwegian and Russian almost at the very summit of modern novel writing, and it is the comparative lack of this distinctive flavor which makes the English and French take a lower place in truth and sincerity.

Everywhere all over the modern European world, men are writing novels and dramas as naturally as the grass or corn or flax grows. The Provençal, the Hun, the Catalonian, the Norwegian, is getting a hearing. This literature is not the literature of scholars; it is the literature of lovers and doers; of men who love the modern and who have not been educated to despise common things.

These men are speaking a new word. They are not hunting themes, they are struggling to express.

Conventional criticism does not hamper or confine them. They are rooted in the soil. They stand among the cornfields and they dig in the peat-bogs. They concern themselves with modern and very present words and themes, and they have brought a new word which is to divide in half the domain of beauty.

They have made art the re-creation of the beautiful *and the significant.* Mere beauty no longer suffices. Beauty is the world-old aristocrat who has taken for mate this mighty young plebeian Significance. Their child is to be the most human and humane literature ever seen.

It has taken the United States longer to achieve independence of English critics than it took to free itself from old-world political and economic rule. Its political freedom was won, not by its gentlemen and scholars, but by its yeomanry; and in the same way our national literature will come in its fulness when the common American rises spontaneously to the expression of his concept of life.

The fatal blight upon most American art has been, and is to-day, its imitative quality, which has kept it characterless and factitious, — a forced rose-culture rather than the free flowering of native plants.

Our writers despised or feared the home market. They rested their immortality upon the "universal theme," which was a theme of no interest to the public and of small interest to themselves.

During the first century and a half, our literature had very little national color. It was quite like the utterance of corresponding classes in England. But at length Bryant and Cooper felt the influence of our mighty forests and prairies. Whittier uttered something of New England boy-life, and Thoreau prodded about among newly discovered wonders, and the American literature got its first start.

Under the influence of Cooper came the stories of wild life from Texas, from Ohio, and from Illinois. The wild, rough settlements could not produce smooth and cultured poems or stories; they only furnished forth rough-and-ready anecdotes, but in these stories there were hints of something fine and strong and native.

As the settlements increased in size, as the pressure of the forest and the wild beast grew less, expression rose to a higher plane; men softened in speech and manner. All preparations were being made for a local literature raised to the level of art.

The Pacific slope was first in the line. By the exceptional interest which the world took in the life of the gold fields, and by the forward urge which seems always to surprise the pessimist and the scholiast, two young men were plunged into that wild life, led across the plains set in the shadow of Mount Shasta, and local literature received its first great marked, decided impetus.

To-day we have in America, at last, a group of writers who have no suspicion of imitation laid upon them. Whatever faults they may be supposed to have, they are at any rate, themselves. American critics can depend upon a characteristic American literature of fiction and the drama from these people.

The corn has flowered, and the cotton-boll has broken into speech.

Local color — what is it? It means that the writer spontaneously reflects the life which goes on around him. It is natural and unstrained art.

It is, in a sense, unnatural and artificial to find an American writing novels of Russia or Spain or the Holy Land. He cannot hope to do it so well as the native. The best he can look for is that poor word of praise, "He does it very well, considering he is an alien."

If a young writer complain that there are no themes at home, that he is forced to go abroad for prospective and romance, I answer there is something wrong in his education or his perceptive faculty. Often he is more anxious to win a money success than to be patiently one of art's unhurried devotees.

I can sympathize with him, however, for criticism has not helped him to be true. Criticism of the formal kind and spontaneous expression are always at war, like the old man and the youth. They may politely conceal it, but they are mutually destructive.

Old men naturally love the past; the books they read are the master-pieces; the great men are all dying off, they say; the young man should treat lofty and universal themes, as they used to do. These localisms are petty. These truths are disturbing. Youth annoys them. Spontaneousness is formlessness, and the criticism that does not call for the abstract and the ideal and the beautiful is leading to destruction, these critics say.

And yet there is a criticism which helps, which tends to keep a writer at his best; but such criticism recognizes the dynamic force of a literature, and tries to spy out tendencies. This criticism to-day sees that local color means national character, and is aiding the young writer to treat his themes in the best art.

I assert it is the most natural thing in the world for a man to love his native land and his native, intimate surroundings. Born into a web of circumstances, enmeshed in common life, the youthful artist begins to think. All the associations of that childhood and the love-life of youth combine to make that web of common affairs, threads of silver and beads of gold; the near-at-hand things are the dearest and sweetest after all.

As the reader will see, I am using local color to mean something more than a forced study of the picturesque scenery of a State.

Local color in a novel means that it has such quality of texture and back-ground that it could not have been writ-

ten in any other place or by any one else than a native.

It means a statement of life as indigenous as the plant-growth. It means that the picturesque shall not be seen by the author, — that every tree and bird and mountain shall be dear and companionable and necessary, not picturesque; the tourist cannot write the local novel.

From this it follows that local color must not be put in for the sake of local color. It must go in, it *will* go in, because the writer naturally carries it with him half unconsciously, or conscious only of its significance, its interest to him.

He must not stop to think whether it will interest the reader or not. He must be loyal to himself, and put it in because he loves it. If he is an artist, he will make his reader feel it through his own emotion.

What we should stand for is not universality of theme, but beauty and strength of treatment, leaving the writer to choose his theme because he loves it.

Here is the work of the critic. Recognizing that the theme is beyond his control, let him aid the young writer to delineate simply and with unwavering strokes. Even here the critic can do little, if he is possessed of the idea that the young writer of to-day should model upon Addison or Macaulay or Swift.

There are new criterions to-day in writing as in painting, and individual expression is the aim. The critic can do much to aid a young writer to *not* copy an old master or any other master. Good criticism can aid him to be vivid and simple and unhackneyed in his technique, the subject is his own affair.

LOCAL COLOR IN ART

I agree with him who says, Local art must be raised to the highest levels in its expression; but in aiding this perfection of technique we must be careful not to cut into the artist's spontaneity. To apply ancient dogmas of criticism to our life and literature would be benumbing to [the] artist and fatal to his art.

VI

THE LOCAL NOVEL

VI. THE LOCAL NOVEL

The local novel seems to be the heir-apparent to the kingdom of poesy. It is already the most promising of all literary attempts to-day; certainly it is the most sincere. It seems but beginning its work. It is "hopelessly contemporaneous;" that is its strength. It is (at its best) unaffected, natural, emotional. It is sure to become all-powerful. It will redeem American literature, as it has already redeemed the South from its conventional and highly wrought romanticism.

By reason of growing truth and sincerity the fiction of the South has risen from the dead. It is now in the spring season of shooting wilding plants and timorous blades of sown grains. Its future is assured. Its soil is fertilized with the blood of true men. Its women are the repositories of great, vital, sincere, emotional experiences which will inevitably appear in their children, and at last in art, and especially in fiction. The Southern people are in the midst of a battle more momentous than the Rebellion, because it is the result of the Rebellion; that is, the battle of intrenched privilege against the swiftly-spreading democratic idea of equality before the law and in the face of nature.

They have a terribly, mightily dramatic race-problem on their hands. The South is the meeting-place of winds. It is the seat of swift and almost incalculable change; and this change, this battle, this strife of invisible powers, is about to enter their fiction.

The negro has already entered it. He has brought a musical speech to his masters, and to the new fiction. He has brought a strange and pleading song into music. The finest writers of the New South already find him a never-failing source of interest. He is not, of course, the only subject of Southern fiction, nor even the principal figure; but he is a necessary part, and a most absorbingly interesting part.

The future of fiction in the South will also depict the unreconstructed rebel unreservedly, and the race-problem without hate or contempt or anger; for the highest art will be the most catholic in its sympathy. It will delineate vast contending forces, and it will be a great literature.

The negro will enter the fiction of the South, first, as subject; second, as artist in his own right. His first attempts will be imitative, but he will yet utter himself, as surely as he lives. He will contribute a poetry and a novel as peculiarly his own as the songs he sings. He may appear, also, in a strange half-song, half-chant, and possibly in a drama peculiar to himself; but in some form of fiction he will surely utter the sombre and darkly-florid genius for emotional utterance which characterizes him.

In the North the novel will continue local for some time to come. It will delineate the intimate life and speech of every section of our enormous and widely scattered republic. It will catch and fix in charcoal the changing, assimilating races, delineating the pathos and humor and the infinite drama of their swift adjustment to new conditions. California, New Mexico, Idaho, Utah, Oregon, each wonderful locality in our Nation of Nations will yet find its native utterance. The superficial work of the tourist and outsider will not do. The real novelist of these sections is walking behind the plow or trudging to school in these splendid potential environments.

This local movement will include the cities as well, and St. Louis, Chicago, San Francisco, will be delineated by artists born of each city, whose work will be so true that it could not have been written by any one from the outside. The real utterance of a city or a locality can only come when a writer is born out of its intimate heart. To such an one, nothing will be "strange" or "picturesque;" all will be familiar, and full of significance or beauty. The novel of the slums must be written by one who has played there as a child, and taken part in all its amusements; not out of curiosity, but out of pleasure seeking. It cannot be done from above nor from the outside. It must be done out of a full heart and without seeking for effect.

The artist should not look abroad to see how others are succeeding. Success does not always measure merit. It took nearly a third of a century for Whitman and Monet to be recognized. The great artist never conforms. He does not trail after some other man's success. He works out his individual perception of things.

The contrast of city and country, everywhere growing sharper, will find its reflection in this local novel of the immediate future, — the same tragedies and comedies, with the essential difference called local color, and taking place all over the land, wherever cities arise like fungi, unhealthy, yet absorbing as subjects of fictional art.

As I have elsewhere pointed out, the drama will join the novel in this study of local conditions. It will be derived from fiction, and in many cases the dramatist and novelist will be the same person. In all cases the sincerity of the author's love for his scenes and characters will find expression in tender care for truth, and there will be made to pass before our eyes wonderfully suggestive pictures of other lives and landscapes. The drama will grow in dignity and importance along these lines.

Both drama and novel will be colloquial. This does not mean that they will be exclusively in the dialects, but the actual speech of the people of each locality will unquestionably be studied more closely than ever before. Dialect is the life of a language, precisely as the common people of the nation form the sustaining power of its social life and art.

And so in the novel, in the short story, and in the drama — by the work of a multitude of loving artists, not by the work of an over-topping personality — will the intimate social, individual life of the nation be depicted. Before this localism shall pass away, such a study will have been made of this land and people as has never been made by any other age or social group, — a literature from the plain people, reflecting their unrestrained outlook on life, subtle in speech and color, humane beyond precedent, humorous, varied, simple in means, lucid as water, searching as sunlight.

To one who believes each age to be its own best interpreter, the idea of "decay of fiction" never comes. That which the absolutist takes for decay is merely change. The conservative fears change; the radical welcomes it. The conservative tries to argue that fundamentals cannot change; that they are the same yesterday, to-day, and tomorrow.

If that were true, then a sorrowful outlook on the future would be natural. Such permanency would be death. Life means change.

As a matter of fact, the minute differentiations of literature which the conservative calls its non-essentials, are really its essentials. Vitality and growth are in these "non-essentials." It is the difference in characters, not their similarity, which is forever interesting. It is the subtle coloring individuality gives which vitalizes landscape art, and so it is the subtle differences in the interpretation of life which each age gives that vitalizes its literature and makes it its own.

The individuality of the artist is the saving grace of art; and landscape painting will not be fantastic so long as men study nature. It will never be mere reproduction so long as the artist represents it as he sees it. The fact will correct the fantasy. The artist will color the fact.

The business of the present is not to express fundamentals, but to sincerely present its own minute and characteristic interpretation of life. This point cannot be too often insisted upon. Unless a writer add something to the literature of his race, has he justification? Is there glory in imitation? Is the painter greatest who copies old masters, or is it more praiseworthy to embody an original conception? These are very important questions for the young artist.

To perceive the hopelessness of absolutism in literature, you have but to stop a moment to think. Admit that there are perfect models to which must be referred all subsequent writing; and we are committed to a barren round of hopeless imitations. The young writer is disheartened or drawn off into imitations, and ruined for any real expression. This way of looking at literature produced our Barlows and Coltons and Hillhouses, with their "colossi of cotton-batting," and it produces blank-verse dramas to-day.

But the relativists in art are full of hope. They see that life is the model, — or, rather, that each man stands accountable to himself first, and to the perceived fact of life second. Life is always changing, and literature changes with it. It never decays; it changes. Poetry — that is to say *impassioned personal outlook on life* — is in no more danger of extinction to-day than in the days of Edmund Spenser. The American novel will continue to grow in truth to American life without regard to the form and spirit of the novel or drama of the past. Consciously or unconsciously, the point of view of the modern writer is that of the veritist, or truth stater.

Once out of the period of tutelage, it is natural for youth to overleap barriers. He naturally discards the wig and cloak of his grandfathers. He comes at last to reject, perhaps a little too brusquely, the models which conservatism regards with awe. He respects them as history, but he has life, abounding, fresh, contiguous life; life that stings and smothers and overwhelms and exalts, like the salt, green, snow-tipped ocean surf; life, with its terrors and triumphs, right here and now; its infinite drama, its allurement, its battle, and its victories. Life is the model, truth is the master, the heart of the man himself his motive power. The pleasure of re-creating in the image of nature is the artist's unfailing reward.

To him who sees that difference, not similarity, is the vitalizing quality, there is no sorrow at change. The future will take care of itself. In the space of that word "difference" lies all the infinite range of future art. Some elements are comparatively unchanging. The snow will fall, spring will come, men and women love, the stars will rise and set, and grass return again and again in vast rhythms of green, but society will not be the same.

The physical conformation of our nation will change. It will lose its wildness, its austerity. Its unpeopled plains will pass away, and gardens will bloom where the hot sand now drifts. Cities will rise where now the elk and the mountain lions are. Swifter means of transportation will bring the lives of different sections into closer relationship. It will tend to equalize intellectual opportunities. The physical and mental life of men and women will be changed, the relation of man to man, and man to woman, will change in detail, and the fiction of the future will express these changes.

To the veritist, therefore, the present is the vital theme. The past is dead, and the future can be trusted to look after itself. The young men and maidens of that time will find the stars of their present brighter than the stars of '92, the people around them more absorbing than books, and their own outlook on life more reasonable than that of dead men. Their writing and painting, in proportion to its vitality and importance, will reflect this, their natural attitude, toward life and history.

VII

THE DRIFT OF THE DRAMA

VII. THE DRIFT OF THE DRAMA

The American drama, from the earliest time of its entry into the colonies, has intensified and carried to the farthest absurdity the principle of dependence upon other times and countries for models. It has reflected at various times Shakespeare, Dryden, Bulwer, Schiller, Sheridan, Scott, and Dickens, not to speak of other and unnameable depths of imitation.

Even when impassioned genius rose to the delineation of native scenes, no landscape was remote enough or wild enough to keep out the tender English maiden and the villain in top-coat and riding-boots. The question of inheritance, the production of lost wills, and the final restoration of the heroine to her own true lover went on quite in the standard British manner.

Once or twice, however, by the sheer force of the subject, conventions were driven out. But these instances simply throw into greater contrast the universal sterility of invention.

Ephemeral dramas of Revolutionary times and plays of American society, wherein the characters were all ticketed as Master Lively, Simon Solemn, or Mistress Long Tongue, abounded up to 1840; the historical dramas of this period were mere spectacles, and had no literary value of any sort.

Historically, the Civil War marks an epoch in the drama, as it does in poetry and the novel. It divided the old from the new, not in abrupt separation, but with the coming of that mighty outburst of national passion the old was thrown

69

into pale obscurity, to linger on for a while, but to lose vitality as the New moved inexorably forward.

The border drama seems to have been the first decided indication of Americanism in the drama. It sprang almost directly from the novel of adventure represented by Cooper and Bird and Webber, and was equally gory. Of this sort was "Tamora" and "Shot in the Eye." [1] However, the tender, fainting maiden and the irreproachable lover were always found in even these mid-forest complications. It had the merit, to be sure, of being in prose, and at times approached a study of life.

Later, the novels of Bret Harte and Joaquin Miller gave a higher turn to these border dramas, and the Indian took a subordinate position, the miner and desperado holding the centre of the stage. As these novels were immensely higher in literary style and arrangement, so the dramas modelled upon them could not entirely escape being touched here and there with truth and poetry.

It is a curious consideration that people will endure, upon the stage, absurdities which would disgust them in the novel. The stage has always been conventional, symbolical, at its best; and the swift movement, the glare of lights, and the atmosphere of artificiality in the decoration, have bewildered the judgment, and made the very worst melodrama disgracefully acceptable to large masses of fairly well educated people.

We find, therefore, a public apparently willing to pay for the worn-out fashions of the novel, sitting with small

---

[1] *Jack Long in Texas; or Shot in the Eye* was produced at the Bowery Theatre, New York City, in March 1879.

uneasiness before dramatic writing which is below the level of even the weekly story papers.

The ambitious "society plays" are for the most part on the level of the "Saturday Evening Romancer." Their heroes never appear without creases in their trousers, and their heroines are actuated by the same characterless and flabby sentiment all heroines have manifested for centuries; and the men and women of both melodrama and society plays appear to be sexually diseased, precisely as in the French novel and the cheap story paper.

Where the technique is better, the outlook on life is hopelessly false and pathologic, — quite on the model of the satyriasic French novelists, who seem to find healthy human feeling a bore, and who scent a suggestive situation with the nostrils of a vulture. Thus, while the American novel has grown steadily more truthful and wholesome, the drama, with several notable exceptions, has kept the low level of imitative English sensationalism and sterile French sexualism.

While the above statement of the low plane of the drama is true in general, there are indubitable signs of change, and change for the better; and it requires little prophetic insight to predict that the drama is soon to take its place beside the novel.

The border drama seems to have lodged at last in the ten cent theatres. The English melodrama is a great deal discredited, almost rejected. The ephemeral farce-comedy seems to be losing its dominion, being superseded on the serious side by character comedy, and on its amusement side by the comic opera, which occasionally really amuses people.

The one-part play still holds a place on the stage, by reason of the survival of the "star," but the public is demanding something more than a monologue. And one by one the one-part plays are discredited and die out. The better public demand[s] a play which shall present in some sort the proportions of art.

Burlesque seems to have been filling in a transition state. When old forms are decaying, they are always food for the satirists. It is not without reason that the farce-comedy writers have held the stage for ten years. They had a work to do, and they have done it merrily and well. It was their business to invalidate the absurd sentiment and false action of the old plays. It is a very good sign to see an audience laugh heartily when the mock heavy villain walks on dragging his toes, and smiling sardonically. The burlesquer has made the strut and shout of old-time tragedy absurd, and has weakened the bonds which kept the school-bred American enslaved to the idea that Shakespeare and the glorious old comedies ended the forms of the drama. The burlesquer respects nothing but the truth, which he cannot distort.

There could be no progress, no native output, so long as the past lay like a brazen wall across the way of the young dramatist. The free untrodden paths do not lie in the direction of the past. Shakespeare and Molière are to be ignored *as models*, precisely as they expressed themselves in youthful unconcern of Æschylus and Sophocles.

The undue worship of Shakespeare or any other dramatist is fatal to individual creation. There can be only one creative model, and that is life. Truth and sincerity of purpose on the part of the writer, if he be of genuinely creative temper, will lead him to the untrod spaces without theory and without slavery.

The American realist should stand for a liberated art. If this means emancipation from Shakespeare, or Scott, or Hugo, very well; but we should not argue for a change of masters. We should condemn with equal severity imitation of a living master like Ibsen.

A work of art is an individual thing, — a relation of one human soul to life, emotionally expressed. The artist will find many having the same outlook substantially, but as an artist he has nothing to do with that. His only obligation is to be true to life as it seems to him from his personal angle of vision.

It may be said again at this point that the past is not vital to the millions of America. Critics of the scholastic sort, with their natural or acquired conservatism, have half-convinced a certain class of Americans (small, in relation to sixty millions of people) that there are dramatic gods in the past, before whom all intellects and especially all creative youth, are to bow down; but the great body of American readers rebel against such intellectual slavery. It needs the illuminating genius of Edwin Booth to make "Hamlet" endurable.[2] These facts are admitted by the

[2] During his early years in Boston Garland frequently attended the performances of Edwin Booth (1833–1893), a tragedian known for his Shakespearean roles. Garland later wrote that "Booth and his Shakespeare were the greatest educative influences in my life at this time." (*Roadside Meetings*, p. 13.)

theatre manager, who has his uses, after all. With him "Shakespeare spells failure." The public prefers "Held by the Enemy" [3] and "The Lost Paradise" [4] and "Shore Acres" [5] to "Hamlet," — which is their privilege.

This has nothing to do with the greatness of Shakespeare any more than it has with the grandeur of Æschylus. It is simply proof that neither of these great figures are part of our lives to-day. They are educational in effect. They illuminate the past with marvellous, inestimable light; but the sorrows of a child, the story of a struggling, hopeless negro, or the parting of an old Hoosier farmer from his daughter, gets closer to us, touches us in a more vital way, than the death of Hamlet or the passion of Clytemnestra.

A perception of these changes in values is necessary to the modern dramatist. Naturally, if he proceeds upon what he believes to be the popular track, without the motive which is absolutely necessary for good art, of expressing his own individual feeling, he must recognize this change of sentiment. The feeling of the average man must be taken into account, rather than the judgment of the pedant.

It may be sorrowful to the student conservative and to the aristocratic party in literature to see old dramatic forms draw off, but to others it is a sign of liberty and of native new birth. It is as natural as the growth of grass. The spontaneous outgrowth of native art may modify old forms, it must not be bound by them.

[3] *Held by the Enemy*, by William Gillette, copyright 1898.
[4] *The Lost Paradise*, adapted from the German of Ludwig Fulda by Henry C. DeMille, was copyrighted in 1897 but produced earlier.
[5] *Shore Acres*, copyright 1890, was written by Garland's friend James A. Herne.

The fight is not between Shakespeare and Sheridan on one side, and the forces represented by Valdes and Ibsen and Howells on the other; it is the immitigable war between creative Youth and reminiscent Age. It is the rebellious demand of youth for the right to utter himself in his own way, without reference to past models. It is youth facing life and the future over against age and aristocracy, clinging to the inheritances of the past, and facing certain death.

Every great group of dramatists in the past, every great change in painting, has met the same opposition; the same anathemas have been winged, the same warnings have been uttered that are now being brought against those who refuse to be bound by the dramatic models of the past, or by the old masters in paint and oil. The veritist accepts as a matter of course the opposition he meets.

The promise of change in the drama is becoming fulfilment in the rapid rise of the local drama, which is following exactly in the line marked out by the local novel; that is to say, the best dramas of American life of the last ten years have risen from the loyal love of the dramatist for certain local phases of American life; and in each case the love of subject has aided the dramatist to override, in some degree, barren conventions, and to produce lifelike groups of characters.

You have but to run over a few of the names to perceive this. "The Old Homestead," [6] "Blue Jeans," [7] "The County

---

[6] *The Old Homestead*, a rural drama of Yankee life by Denman Thompson and George W. Ryder, copyright 1885.
[7] *Bluejeans*, by Joseph Arthur, copyright 1888.

Fair," [8] "Alabama," "Shore Acres," "In Mizzoura," [9] etc.

It must here again be repeated that the radical critic often takes interest in some art output, not because it is a perfect product, a rounded masterpiece of imitation of some model, but because it indicates a desire for change; because it prophesies new things.

He praises "Shore Acres," "Alabama," and "In Mizzoura" because they are significant of change from melodrama to native character comedy. They are leaves, showing the set of the current. Where the actuating motive of the dramatist is to celebrate some life he has lived and loved, the traditions of the drama count for less; truth counts for more.

Instances of this are to be seen in Mr. Herne's "Shore Acres" and "In Mizzoura," by Augustus Thomas. Mr. Herne's "Shore Acres" has not only opened a new dispensation in New England drama, but by its great money success will encourage all other dramatists working upon local themes. It more nearly approaches the delineation of New England life than any other play to date. It rises in some scenes nearly to the level of Miss Wilkins's stories.

Veritism is unquestionably acting upon the drama as impressionism has already transformed painting, and changed the current of literature. Veritism discredits plots and formal complications. It deals with life face to face, and swiftly and surely and always from the individual artist's standpoint. Characters and the relation of groups of characters are coming to have more value than plot.

[8] *The County Fair; or the Country Fair*, by Charles Barnard and Neil Burgess, copyright 1890.
[9] Both *Alabama* (1891), a dramatic attempt to reconcile North and South, and *In Mizzoura* (1893) were written by Augustus Thomas.

When Mr. Howells remarked upon this some years ago, the walls of Jericho were apparently shaken down, to judge from the dust and noise of reverberating explosion. Managers, secure in possession of the "Crimes of London" [10] and the "Gaslights of Paris," turned the American dramatist out on the street, through the medium of their suave black porters. As several of them plainly said, they had no use for American dramatists. But to-day every marked and continued success on our stage is an American drama of character, treated with more or less of sincerity and truth.

Everywhere the value of truth increases, not only from the literary side of the stage, but from its commercial side. Mr. Harrigan's character sketches of New York low life will be supplemented or superseded by character studies of all classes of New York society. Mr. Brander Matthews, Mr. Clyde Fitch, and Mr. Richard Harding Davis are likely to make finished and valuable contributions to local New York drama.

Mr. Joel Harris is writing a drama of the South. Mr. Cable is reported to be dramatizing one of his novels. Miss Wilkins has made a most excellent beginning with "Giles Corey." [11] She will do better when she handles a modern theme. Without question, the local novelists and the local dramatists are to be co-workers in future, and the whole outlook is very fine and promising.

Our stage is soon to be filled with the most amusing and interesting, because truthful and most human characters

[10] *The Crimes of London*, a melodrama by Charles De Kress, copyright 1884.

[11] Mary E. Wilkins's play, *Giles Corey* (1893), treated the Salem witchcraft trials.

ever grouped on any one national stage. Every vitally interesting theme will find its dramatists, for there is no set law for the form and theme of the drama.

There is only one law for the dramatist: *he must interest his audience from start to finish*. Interest does not mean merely to amuse. The stage cannot long remain a mere amusement. It must interest and instruct as well, or it will pall upon the public palate like a diet of honey or vinegar. Public taste changes with great rapidity, making conditions which seem stable vanish like smoke.

Less than five years ago we were lost in a tumult of English melodrama. Every theatre echoed with the voices of the hero and the heavy villain. We seem likely to begin the next season practically without the aid of cheap English drama, and more and better American plays are promised than at any other time in the history of our drama.

Taste is certainly rising to meet the dramatist, who was on the higher levels long before the public (or, at least, before the manager), waiting impatiently a chance to put his best work before the world. His chance seems coming at last.

VIII

THE INFLUENCE OF IBSEN

VIII. THE INFLUENCE OF IBSEN

In this transition stage the works of Henrik Ibsen are coming to have great significance. No doubt there is a good deal of manufactured admiration current, but there is enough of genuine enthusiasm to make his ideas and works an issue. His significance is very great.

He not only represents a distinctive phase of dramatic writing, but he stands (consciously) for the idea of progress in art. He stands for actuality. He is consistently and wholly progressive, and may be taken to represent the whole movement in dramatic art commonly called realism, but which might be called "modernism."

Realism, in its true sense, in the sense in which the Spanish novelist Valdes uses it, and as Mr. Howells uses it, does not mean the reproduction in a drama of tanks and fire-engines, or real burglars blowing open a safe. Neither does realism in the novel mean the study of murderers, insane or criminal classes. Realism in its broadest meaning is simply the idea of perceiving and stating the truth in an individual way, irrespective of past models. It is progress in art. It does not despise the past, but, on the other hand, it does not accept any man or age as model.

Ibsen, the great Norwegian poet and dramatist, having become an issue in the drama, the study of his methods is likely to yield good results.

He is a realist first, in his choice of theme. He is not content with the themes common to dramas. He deals with life, and modern life, — primarily with Norwegian life, but with the life of other lands secondarily, for the reason that his theme is common and modern, and his aim truth. The passions, situations of his drama, appeal to us as real, because they are actualities of his land and time.

He is modern, in that his domain is one upon which no dramatist of the Elizabethan or of the romantic German age has ever trenched. Values in his plays are readjusted to suit modern life. He not only treats of modern themes, but gives the modern man's comment upon them.

Thus his choice of motive in itself announces a widening of the domain of the drama. No longer restricted to the cardinal passions, — love, fear, hate, jealousy, or revenge, — all emotions, and especially all new, distinctively modern and intellectual emotions, are to be used as basis for the coming drama.

Life is to be depicted, not love-life. Sexual attractions and perplexities do not form life, but only *part* of life. Even the old passions are taking new forms. Ambition concerns itself with new objects, and hate has new expressions. Life is in continual process of change, and in conformity to these social and individual changes the drama always has changed and must ever change.

Ibsen's work not only predicts the impending change; it enforces it. His themes could not have been used by any other age; in no past age would they have been understood, — nor are they now, for a vast and electric prophecy runs through them all.

It is an advanced condition of mind, an exceptional mental development that enables Ibsen to find poetry and significance in the realities of modern life. He was born a reformer. His plays are not merely radical in theory, they are sections of life, — segments, not circles; for nothing begins or ends in this world. All is ebb and flow. It is only in the romance that things are finished, rounded out, and smoothed down.

His realities are, moreover, common realities. Take "The Enemy of Society," for example, perhaps the most radical in form and subject (dramatically) of all his plays. See how small a part the passion of love or jealousy plays in it! See how great a part pure intellect plays!

The theme is sociological. The treatment so magnificently direct and masterly, the characterization so honest, we are made to feel very near these townsmen whose secret feelings and thoughts are being laid bare to us. Note what wide representative reach has been attained by being faithful to actual conditions. It might all have happened at Bar Haven or at Boomtown, Nebraska. The same lying, booming, robbing goes on where the social conditions are similar, the same deceits and corruptions; being true to the Norwegian village, he attains the widest interest.

I repeat, he is a realist in his choice of subject, because he treats of ideas, emotions, and situations new to the drama but common to life, and deals with them all in a new way. We are done with machinery, fustian, and claptrap as we enter his dramatic world. Worn-out themes have no place in the six or seven social dramas he has given us.

How true and unconventional his style. We hardly realize how false and stilted current stage-conversation is, till we hear the real word spoken there. His words come to us at times like thrust of naked fists. They shake the hearer with their weight of real passion. In one sense this speech is astoundingly direct, and then again it is subtly indirect — as in life. Observe how his lovemaking proceeds. How chary of words. Only a hint here and there. Its expression is left mainly to the tone of the voice, or put into the vibrant undertone when talking of the weather, or it is dramatized in the face.

For example, see Hovstadt with Petra in "The Enemy of Society." As in life, where the word "love" means most it is used charily; especially is this true among the middle classes. On the stage, however, it is so common as to lose all significance and sacredness.

Observe also that in the superb reality of his plays the soliloquy is lost, that hoary monstrosity; that cheap way of explaining to the audience what the dramatist had not the skill to suggest; that ancient device, by which the hero tells the gallery that his heart is breaking, while the villain explains the plot and unfolds his wickedness! The soliloquy, the stronghold of the conventional drama, is gone when we enter the theatre where Ibsen's later plays are being performed.

Verity demands, also, simplicity of plan. Observe this in "The Doll-Home," in "Ghosts," in "Rosmersholm." No complications, no external intricacies, hardly anything approaching a plot, the interest depending entirely upon the characterization and the thought. The pursuit and not the end, has become (as in the novel) the leading motive.

The plan springs from the characters, and unrolls mysteriously, with all the unforeseen changes of life itself. Nothing can be foretold any more than in a novel of life.

At his best he takes a common man or a representative man
and follows him through a moral or mental change, with
all his logical connections, and leaves him as abruptly as he
began.

There are no heroines, villains, and heroes in these un-
compromising dramas. Their race is run. The accom-
modating gentleman who keeps things stirred up through
four acts in order that the hero may display himself, is
out of business in this modern drama. Krogstadt is the
nearest approach to this factotum, the villain, and he is
only a man gone wrong, and persecuting, not for love of
it, but for love of his children, — persecution based on the
affection of a father and not on lust and greed.

This brings me to one of the greatest distinctions of all,
and that is the dramatist's treatment of motives. One hardly
dares say how much this may come to mean to the realist.
Nothing shows the great Norwegian's power of delineation and his love for verity and for justice more clearly
than his treatment of the moving forces of his characters.
He sees them completely in form and dress, speech and
motive. They are men and women.

As one reads "Pillars of Society," for example, following
the study of Bernick, it seems at first like a merciless satire,
— but wait and see! The drama mounts at length into the
region of motives. It tells that the hypocrite Bernick is himself a product of conditions. He has his side of the story,
and the power to state it well-nigh irresistibly. "Perhaps
you think I acted from selfish motives," Bernick pleads.
"If I had stood alone, then, I would have begun the world
again, cheerfully and bravely. But you don't understand

how the head of a great house becomes a living part of the business he inherits, with its enormous responsibility. Do you know that the weal or woe of thousands depends upon him?"

LONA. — It is for the sake of the community then, that for these fifteen years you have stood upon a lie?

BERNICK. — A lie?

LONA. — I call it the lie, — the threefold lie.

BERNICK. — Would you have me sacrifice my domestic happiness and my position in society?

LONA. — What right have you to stand where you are standing?

BERNICK. — I've gained more and more right every day for fifteen years, — by all I've labored for, by my whole life, by all I've won.

We begin to ponder; we ask ourselves whether we would have done better had we been in his place.

Thus each character has, in a sense, his justification. We see things from their standpoint. The fluent and all-embracing sympathy of the dramatist has gone around these men and women. Malformed and twisted as they are, they have always a *dramatic* justification for their action.

We come now to his dramatic situations, where again his faithfulness to fact is shown. In life, how slight a thing leads to a tragedy! A misapprehension, a feeling of foolish pride, a jest, a word or two spoken hastily, — these are the causes of many a life-long separation, many a tragic sorrow. Considered from the stage, how slight is the barrier between Nora and Thorvald in "The Doll-Home," but how insuperable considered from the standpoint of life.

86

We have a difference arising between the brothers Stockman in "The Enemy of Society," — a difference based upon deep mental disagreements, upon fundamental facts, and which will separate them forever.

There is something recognizably immitigable in these terrible moods. They shake us, for we recognize our own liability to such disasters; but in the melodrama and the romantic play, no matter what happens, we remain tranquil. Though the heroine be burned at the stake, and the hero thrice set upon, we know that through flame and bolt, and wastes of sea, in spite of hate and purchased justice, they will come forth vindicated and unharmed in the joyous fifth act. We know this, and feel about for our overshoes.

But in the plays of Ibsen we do not find ourselves able to predict what changes may come, for the reason that the action springs from and depends upon the characters. The full meaning of this may not appear at first sight. To have the action spring from the characters is to destroy the traditional plot. It means to have individuals, not situations. It means that this is the farthest present remove from the immitigable doom in Æschylus, and the fixed complications of Shakespearian comedy. It destroys romantic plots and under-plots.

On the same general principle of verity first and effect afterwards, is Ibsen's superb treatment of what are called irrelevant characters, irrelevant incident. He selects certain characters for delineation, and then uses such others as naturally come into the range of his drama; and as the action passes on and leaves them behind, they do not reappear. They served their purpose and are lost to view.

The dramatist takes two or three life-lines, which he holds in his hands, and, like the novelist, traces them through the maze of incident. For example, in "The Doll-Home" there are two central figures; around them are changing groups of men and women. The hearer or reader feels that these people are a part of life, that other men and women meet and influence them for a time and pass out of their lives. Only the few are in any way accounted for at the end.

This is in accordance with the ideas put by Olive Schreiner into that strange and powerful preface to "An African Farm":

Human life may be painted according to two methods. There is the stage method. According to that, each character is duly marshalled at first and ticketed. We know with an immutable certainty that at the right crises each will reappear, act his part, and when the curtain falls all will stand before it bowing. There is a sense of satisfaction in this and completeness. But there is another method, the method of the life we lead. Here nothing can be prophesied. There is a strange coming and going of feet. Men appear, act, and react upon each other and pass away. When the crisis comes, the man who would fit it does not appear. When the curtain falls, no one is ready. . . . Life may be painted according to either method, but the methods are different. The canons of criticism that bear upon the one, cut cruelly across the other.

Here is the creed, if creed it may be called, of the absolute veritist or realist. Ibsen may be criticised, but only with reference to this principle of verity. If there is irrelevant incident in life, then it does not belong to the drama. There are no traditional criterions by which to judge a man whose aim is, not to conform to traditions, but to ignore them.

See the power of an "irrelevant character" in Dr. Rank! Apparently unrelated, yet what power lies in his coming and going. Nothing in the play seemed to me more irresistibly courageous and true than the handling of that modern man.

But *was* he irrelevant? Is he not subtly related? Does he not throw into relief the life, the abounding animality, of Thorvald and the unthinking happiness of Nora? He seems to me deeply significant as a foil, such as we see in daily life, when the dead lie silently in the dim room, —

> And the summer morning is cool and sweet,
> And we hear the live folk laugh in the street.

Every character we note closely stands in a subtle relation to us in real life, and every character which comes naturally into the drama of verities has significance. The traditional law that it must "help the story on" has no significance where the story is lost sight of in the development of character, where the pursuit and not the end is the first consideration, as with the realist.

On the score of pure modernness, originality, and truth, both in subject and method, I am inclined to put "The Enemy of Society" at the head of the dramas I have read of the great Norwegian. It is the most modern, the most unconventional, the most radical, and, to me, one of the most powerful dramas ever written. Love plays in it but the small part it should; other ideas and emotions absorb us. Like a section of life, it has no beginning and no end. It has no machinery, and nothing is forced. It is as modern as the telephone.

"Yes, and as lacking in beauty," says some one. "To *you*," I reply; "to me it has something that is higher than beauty; it has truth."

Using the same criterion, life, we see that "The Pillars of Society" is not quite so modern. It has a little of the machinery of the stage left. Things *happen* here and there, but it is powerfully unconventional, for all that. It is filled with superb living figures, and the treatment of Bernick is beyond praise. A powerful satire, it does not fail of doing justice to each figure.

Finally, Ibsen's treatment of woman stamps his radical departure from old standards more clearly, perhaps, than any other point. The feudalistic woman has been for centuries either a sovereign or a servant, a heroine or a drudge. In the ordinary drama she is long-suffering, patient, and beautiful, or is pretty and provokes laughter.

Predominantly, from the days of Edmund Spenser to the last issue of the dime novel, the heroine has been characterless, colorless, and passive. In the romantic drama she has languished in dungeons, been the passive subject of duels and abductions, calumny, and reproach. She has been deceived, driven from home, cheated of her inheritance, schemed for by villains, and rescued by heroes, while gazing with big round eyes at the world which was a chaos of crime and wickedness. Her bodily allurements have been harped upon and exaggerated till she has imagined the whole world eager to possess her, warring only for her. It is impossible to estimate the harm this sort of lying has produced.

To pass from such an atmosphere to that of Ibsen's plays is like going from a questionable ballroom, filled with painted and simpering faces, out into the crisp bracing air of the street, filled with healthy and vigorous men and women; like going into a home where man and wife, equal in fact as in law, are discussing the questions of the day with a party of valued friends. And yet in the feudalistic picture there was once [a] large element of truth. It is no longer true; it should be discarded. A new woman has appeared in life.

Dramatically, Ibsen's women are centres of action; not passive dramatic "bones of contention," but *active agents in their turn.* Indeed, they take the play in their own hands at times. They re-act upon men, they rise above men at times in the perception of justice, of absolute ethics; they are out in the world, the men's world. They may not understand it very well, but they are at least in it, and having their opinion upon things, and voicing their emotions. They are out of the unhealthy air of the feudalistic romance, so much is certain, so much is gain. They are grappling, not merely with affairs, but with social problems.

My criticism of Ibsen in this particular is again on the score of reality. In his rebound from the false and degrading pictures of women as having but one life, love-life, he has, in my estimation, used too large a proportion of remarkable women to be perfectly true to his time and country; and in order to emphasize the growing power and expanding individuality of the modern woman, he has once or twice included the improbable, if not the impossible, in the action of his women.

There is also a strain of morbid psychology in many of his characters which I do not value. I prefer his studies of more common phases of modern intellectual life. Yet the whole outcome of even these studies of morbid conditions is helpful, fine, and strong, and he does not lose his grasp on surrounding facts, when studying these special cases.

It is a trite saying that the sense of humor is a "saving

157140

grace." This element is not lacking in Ibsen, but it is not so well developed as to give that peculiar touch of saving grace. There is a plenty of grim humor, but there is little of *kindly* humor in his plays. He is kept from being extravagant not by the sense of the ridiculous so much as by sheer intellect and deep vibrant sympathy. The humor that is everywhere a corrective in the fervid sympathy and burning social discontent of Mr. Howells's later novels is not found in Ibsen; and, lacking it, "The Doll-Home" lacks the fine poise a humorous sense of human frailties gives to a serious work of fiction.

One closes a reading of these astounding dramas with the consciousness that something electric has passed by. They stand so sheer above most of the dramas of the age that it is no wonder the critics are amazed and enraged. The person who comes to like these dramas and their methods is likely to find his taste for conventional heroics disturbed, if not destroyed. The romantic absurdities of the day cannot flourish long in the same atmosphere. Ibsen is a great herald, his dramas lead to the future.

Observe, I do not claim for him superhuman merit. These plays are not the farther wall. They are not yet on a plane with the great novels of the day. Their purpose is too obvious, but they are a superb advance. Ibsen already sees the beauty and significance of the common life of the day. He begins to recognize no such thing as "commonplace." He exemplifies the magnificent sayings of Tolstoy, Valdes, and Whitman, all using almost the same words.

"In nature there is nothing either great or small, all is equal. All is equally great, equally just, equally beautiful.

To talk of the trifles of life is not possible to him who has meditated on the great problem of existence. The trifle does not exist absolutely, only as a relative term. That which is a trifle to some is a great fact to others. In all that is particular we may be shown the general, in all that is finite the infinite. Art is charged with its revelation."

Realism is not a theory, it is a condition of mind, of sensibility. The realist has only one law, to be true to himself; only one criterion, life. He must love genuinely what he depicts, and be true. Anything that he loves, the artist will make important to others as to himself. He must not be discouraged if the general public does not love the same fact as himself. He will find sympathizers at last.

If there is one great idea dominant in the present age, it is this: "Art is not the reproduction of art; each epoch must have its own art." Each age writes, paints, sings of its own time and for its time. All genuine modern art must conform to this general and inexorable law.

Ibsen has helped us in our war against conventionalisms, but he must not dominate us. His plays are not to be models. Our drama will be more human, more wholesome, and more humorous.

IX

IMPRESSIONISM

IX. IMPRESSIONISM

Every competent observer who passed through the art palace at the Exposition was probably made aware of the immense growth of impressionistic or open-air painting. If the Exposition had been held five years ago, scarcely a trace of the blue-shadow idea would have been seen outside the work of Claude Monet, Pisarro, and a few others of the French and Spanish groups.

To-day, as seen in this wonderful collection, impressionism as a principle has affected the younger men of Russia, Norway, Sweden, Denmark, and America as well as the *plein air* school of Giverney.[1] Its presence is put in evidence to the ordinary observer in the prevalence of blue or purple shadows, and by the abundance of dazzling sun-light effects.

This growth of an idea in painting must not be confounded with a mere vogue. It is evolutionary, if not destructive, in the eyes of the old-school painters, at least. To the younger men it assumes almost as much importance as the law of gravity. With them it is the true law of light and shade.

It may be worth while to consider, quite apart from technical terms, the principles upon which this startling departure from the conventional manner is based.

The fundamental idea of the impressionists, as I understand it, is that a picture should be a unified impression. It should not be a mosaic, but a complete and of course momentary concept of the sense of sight. It should not deal

[1] The *plein-air* realists, inspired by Millet, painted peasants out-of-doors in their natural surroundings. Artists of this school include Jules Breton, Rosa Bonheur, and Léon L'hermitte.

with the concepts of other senses (as touch), nor with judgments; it should be the stayed and reproduced effect of a single section of the world of color upon the eye. It should not be a number of pictures enclosed in one frame, but a single idea impossible of subdivision without loss.

They therefore strive to represent in color an instantaneous effect of light and shade as presented by nature, and they work in the open air necessarily. They are concerned with atmosphere always. They know that the landscape is never twice alike. Every degree of the progress of the sun makes a new picture. They follow the most splendid and alluring phases of nature, putting forth almost superhuman effort to catch impressions of delight under which they quiver.

They select some moment, some centre of interest, — generally of the simplest character. This central object they work out with great care, but all else fades away into subordinate blur of color, precisely as in life. We look at a sheep, for example, feeding under a tree. We see the sheep with great clearness, and the tree and the stump, but the fence and hill outside the primary circle of vision are only obscurely perceived. The meadow beyond is a mere blue of yellow-green. This is the natural arrangement. If we look at the fence or the meadow, another picture is born.

It will thus be seen that these men are veritists in the best sense of the word. They are referring constantly to nature. If you look carefully at the Dutch painters and the English painters of related thought, you will find them working out each part of the picture with almost the same clearness. Their canvases are not single pictures, they are mosaics of pictures, packed into one frame. Values are almost equal everywhere.

This idea of impressionism makes much of the relation and interplay of light and shade, — not in black and white, but in color. Impressionists are, above all, colorists. They cannot sacrifice color for multiple lines. They do not paint leaves, they paint masses of color; they paint the *effect* of leaves upon the eye.

They teach that the retina perceives only plane surfaces. The eye takes note, in its primary impressions, of masses rather than lines. This idea affects the painting of groups; and the most advanced painter never loses the unity of light effects, no matter how tempting a subject may be, nor how complex.

This may be illustrated by reference to a picture exhibited in the Norwegian section, — "The First Communion."[2] The scene is the sitting or dining room of a well-to-do family. It is lighted by a single hanging-lamp. The family stand in a semi-circle against the wall. The minister stands silhouetted against the light of the lamp. He is the principal figure of the group, and yet, because truth demanded his position there, he remains a shadow, — but a luminous shadow, kindly, dignified, and authoritative.

The lamp casts blue-green and orange streaks and blurs of color across the table, and over the white shirts and collars. Some of the faces are vague masses of light, wonderfully full of character. Few faces are outlined definitely.

[2] Garland apparently refers to "Confirmation Banquet" by Nils Gustav Wentzel (1859–1927). A picture entitled "First Communion" by A. H. Bramtot of France was exhibited at the Chicago World's Fair, but it does not fit Garland's description.

The whole is simply a splendid and solemn impression, as if in passing by in the darkness one had caught, through an open door, a glance at a hushed and reverential communion ceremony. It is like Dagnan-Bouveret with better color.

Without pointing out, as one might, conspicuous examples of the literal delineation of groups (in the American section as well as elsewhere), I would call attention to the fact that this is the modern picture. It is also the dramatic picture, because it takes up and relates at a stroke the impression of a dramatic moment. The mosaic is the untrue picture because the eye never sees all faces with equal clearness, especially at a moment of dramatic interest.

This singleness of impression destroys, of course, all idea of "cooked up" pictures, as the artists say. There are, moreover, no ornate or balanced effects. The painter takes a swift glance at a hill-side, whose sky-line cuts the picture diagonally, perhaps. It has a wind-blown tuft of trees upon it, possibly. A brook comes into the foreground casually. Or he takes for subject a hay-stack in a field, painting it for the variant effects of sun-light. He finds his heart's-full of beauty and mystery in a bit of a meadow with a row of willows.

He takes intimate views of nature; but if he painted the heart of the Andes, he would do it, not as the civil engineer sees it, but as he himself sees it and loves it.

The second principle, and the one most likely to be perceived by the casual observer, is the use of "raw" colors. The impressionist does not believe nature needs toning or harmonizing. Her colors, he finds, are primary, and are laid on in juxtaposition. Therefore the impressionist does not mix his paints upon his palette. He paints with nature's colors, — red, blue, and yellow; and he places them fearlessly on the canvas side by side, leaving the eye to mix them, as in nature.

For example, the late Dennis M. Bunker, in painting a meadow stream, did not hesitate to paint the water blue as the sky, nor to paint the red band of rust-like silt on the margin of the stream in close juxtaposition to the vivid green of the meadow grass. This picture, beside a Dutch or English conventional landscape, was as radically different, as radiantly beautiful, as a sunlit day in New England June put over against a dull day on the low-lands of the North Sea; and this is right. The painter was not accountable to the Dutch or English or French painters of any time or place; he was accountable only to nature and to his own sense.

This placing of red, blue, and yellow side by side gives a crispness and brilliancy, and a peculiar vibratory quality to sky and earth which is unknown to the old method. And if the observer will forget conventions and will refer the canvas back to nature instead, he will find this to be the true concept.

I once asked a keen lover of nature who knew nothing about painting, to visit a gallery with me and see some impressionistic works which had shocked the city. I asked him to stand before these pictures and tell me just what he thought of them.

He looked long and earnestly, and then turned with an enthusiastic light in his eyes, "That is June grass under the sunlight."

His eyes had not been educated to despise the vigor and splendor of nature. He cared nothing for Corot or Constable or Turner. I believe that the unspoiled perception of a lover of untempered nature will find in the pictures of the best impressionists the quality he calls "natural."

To most eyes the sign-manual of the impressionist is the blue shadow. And it must be admitted that too many impressionists have painted as if the blue shadow were the only distinguishing sign of the difference between the new and the old. The gallery-trotter, with eyes filled with dead and buried symbolisms of nature, comes upon Bunker's meadows, or Sinding's mountain-tops, or Larson's[3] sunsets, and exclaims, "Oh, see those dreadful pictures! Where did they get such colors."

To see these colors is a development. In my own case, I may confess, I got my first idea of colored shadows from reading one of Herbert Spencer's essays ten years ago. I then came to see blue and grape-color in the shadows on the snow. By turning my head top-side down, I came to see that shadows falling upon yellow sand were violet, and the shadows of vivid sunlight falling on the white of a macadamized street were blue, like the shadows on snows.

Being so instructed, I came to catch through the corners of my eyes sudden glimpses of a radiant world which vanished as magically as it came. On my horse I caught glimpses of this marvellous land of color as I galloped across some bridge. In this world stone-walls were no longer cold gray, they were warm purple, deepening as the sun westered.

[3] Garland probably means Carl Glof Larsson (1853–1919), who exhibited a painting, "'Ulf' in the Sunset" at the Chicago World's Fair.

And so the landscape grew radiant year by year, until at last no painter's impression surpassed my world in beauty.

As I write this, I have just come in from a bee-hunt over Wisconsin hills, amid splendors which would make Monet seem low-keyed. Only Enneking and some few others of the American artists, and some of the Norwegians have touched the degree of brilliancy and sparkle of color which was in the world to-day. Amid bright orange foliage, the trunks of beeches glowed with steel-blue shadows on their eastern side. Sumach flamed with marvellous brilliancy among deep cool green grasses and low plants untouched by frost. Everywhere amid the red and orange and crimson were lilac and steel-blue shadows, giving depth and vigor and buoyancy which Corot never saw (or never painted), — a world which Inness does not represent. Enneking comes nearer, but even he tones unconsciously the sparkle of these colors.

Going from this world of frank color to the timid apologies and harmonies of the old-school painters is depressing. Never again can I find them more than mere third-hand removes of nature. The Norwegians come nearer to seeing nature as I see it than any other nationality. Their climate must be somewhat similar to that in which my life has been spent, but they evidently have more orange in their sunlight.

The point to be made here is this, the atmosphere and coloring of Russia is not the atmosphere of Holland. The atmosphere of Norway is much clearer and the colors more vivid than in England. One school therefore cannot copy or be based upon the other without loss. Each painter should paint his own surroundings, with nature for his teacher, rather than some Dutch master, painting the never-ending mists and rains of the sea-level.

This brings me to my settled conviction that art, to be vital, must be local in its subject; its universal appeal must be in its working out, — in the way it is done. Dependence upon the English or French groups is alike fatal to fresh, individual art.

The impressionist is not only a local painter, in choice of subject he deals with the present. The impressionist is not an historical painter, he takes little interest in the monks and brigands of the Middle Ages. He does not feel that America is without subjects to paint because she has no castles and donjon keeps. He loves nature, not history. His attitude toward nature is a personal one. He represents the escape from childish love of war and the glitter of steel.

The impressionist paints portraits and groups, but paints them as he sees them, not as others see them. He has no receipt for "flesh color." He never sees human flesh unrelated in its color, it is always affected by other colors. He paints the yellow hair of a child with red, blue, and yellow, the gray hair of the grandmother with the same primary colors, and attains such truth and vigor that the portraits made with brown shadows seem dull and flat. Observe some of the portraits by Bunker, by Zorn, by Bertha Wegmann and Mrs. Perry, or the figures in firelight by Benson or Tarbell, and you find them all subtle studies of the interplay of color, with no hard and fast line between colors. The face gives to the dress, the dress to the face.

True, these pictures are not calculated for study with a magnifying glass. Meissonier and Detaille always seem to me to partake of the art which carves a coach-and-four out of walnuts; and there are a great many estimable folk who think paintings are to be smelled of, in order to test their quality. Everything is not worked out in these impressionist groups; there is the suggestion of a true impression in their technical handling.

Their work is not hasty, however. It is the result of hard study. They work rapidly, but not carelessly. They are like skilled musicians; the actual working out of the melody is rapid, but it has taken vast study and practice. Lines are few, colors simple, but they are marvellously exact. It must never be forgotten that they are not delineating a scene; they are painting a personal impression of a scene, which is vastly different.

The impressionist does not paint Cherubs and Loves and floating iron chains. He has no conventional pictures, full of impossible juxtapositions. He takes fresh, vital themes, mainly out-of-door scenes. He aims always at freshness and vigor.

The impressionist is a buoyant and cheerful painter. He loves the open air, and the mid-day sun. He has little to say about the "mystery" and "sentiment" of nature. His landscapes quiver with virile color. He emphasizes (too often over-emphasizes) his difference in method, by choosing the most gorgeous subjects. At his worst, the impressionist is daring in his choice of subject and over-assertive in his handling. Naturally, in his reaction he has swung back across the line too far.

This leads Monet to paint the same haystack in twenty different lights, in order to emphasize the value of color and atmosphere over mere subject. It leads Dodge McKnight to paint water "till it looks as if skinned," as one critic said. It led Bunker to paint the radiant meadows of June, and leads Remington to paint the hot hollows between hills of yellow sand, over which a cobalt, cloudless sky arches.

The impressionist, if he is frank, admits the value, historically, of the older painters, but also says candidly, "They do not represent me." I walked through the loan exhibition with a man who cared nothing for precedent, — a keen, candid man; and I afterward visited the entire gallery with a painter, — a strong and earnest man, who had grown out of the gray-black-and-brown method.

Both these men shook their heads at Inness, Diaz, Corot, Troyon, Rousseau, and Millet. The painter said, a little sadly, as if surrendering an illusion, "They do not represent nature to me any more. They're all too indefinite, too weak, too lifeless in shadow. They reproduce beautifully, but their color is too muddy and cold."

The other man was not even sad. He said, "I don't like them, — that's all there is about it. I don't see nature that way. Some of them are decorative, but they are not nature. I prefer Monet or Hassam or the Norwegians."

As for me, these paintings have no power or influence on my life, other than to make me feel once more the inexorable march of art. I respect these men, — they were such deep and tender souls! They worked so hard and so long to embody their conception of nature, but they do not represent me, do not embody the sunlight and shadow I see. They conceived too much, they saw too little. The work of a man like Enneking or Steele or Remington, striving to paint native scenes, and succeeding, is of more interest to me than Diaz.

It is blind fetichism, timid provincialism, or commercial greed which puts the works of "the masters" above the living, breathing artist. Such is the power of authority that people who feel no answering thrill from some smooth, dim old paintings are afraid to say they do not care for them for fear some one will charge them with stupidity or ignorance.

The time is coming when the tyranny of such criticism will be overthrown. There is no exclusive patent on painting. There are just as faithful artists to-day as ever lived, and much more truthful than any past age could have been. Day by day the old sinks an inch. The same questions face the painter that face the novelist or the sculptor. Has the last word been said? Did the masters utter the last word? Are there no new kingdoms of art? It is the age-worn demand of the old that the new shall conform.

The old masters saw nature in a certain way, — right or wrong it does not matter; youth must conform. They saw nature in a sombre fashion, therefore youth must be decorous. Youth, in impressionism, to-day is saying, "I have nothing to do with Constable or Turner. Their success or failure is nothing to me, as an artist. It is my own impression of nature I am to paint, not theirs. I am to be held accountable to nature, not to the painters of a half-century ago.

"If I see plum-colored shadows on the snow, or violet shadows on the sand; if the clouds seen above perpendicular cliffs seem on edge; if a town on a hill in a wild wind seems to lean, then I am to paint it so. I am painting my love for nature, not some other's perception. If this is iconoclasm, I cannot help it."

Very similarly, the tyranny of the classic in sculpture is giving way, and America is beginning to do the work she can do best. Very probably, sculpture will yet embody in stone and bronze the scenes we all love in American life. John Rogers, in his timid way, pointed the way after all. Lanceray, the Russian sculptor, won great fame by embodying, in a way never before realized, the habits and dress of his native land. Theatrical at times, but accurate and swift and unified always, he certainly has demonstrated that a mighty future exists for sculpture, once the tyranny of the Greek is overthrown.

There are few limitations to sculpture. Whatever the artist loves and wishes to put into bronze or marble, that is allowable. All things point toward *genre* sculpture, colored to the life, not conventionally painted, as in Greek art, when sculpture was but just detached from architecture. Wherever the freed soul of the sculptor loves most, there will his eager hand create in the image of his passion.

Our wild animals have already found a great artist in Kemeys. The Indian and the negro also are being spiritedly handled, but the workman in his working clothes, the brakeman, the thresher on the farm, the heater at the furnace, the cow-boy on his horse, the young man in the haying field, offer equally powerful and characteristic subjects. There are no traditional limitations to sculpture. Whatever the sculptor loves and desires to fashion, that is his best possible subject.

The iconoclast is a necessity. He it is who breaks out of the hopeless circle of traditional authority. His declaration of independence is a disturbance to those who sleep on the bosom of the dead prophets. The impressionist is unquestionably an iconoclast, and the friends of the dead painters are properly alarmed. Here, as everywhere, there are the two parties, — the one standing for the old, the other welcoming the new. A contest like that between realism and romanticism is not playful, it is destructive.

To a man educated in the school of Munich, the pictures, both of the Norwegian and of the Giverney group of Frenchmen and all other pictures with blue and purple shadows, are a shock. They are not merely variants, they are flags of anarchy; they leave no middle ground, apparently. If they are right, then all the rest are wrong. By contrast the old is slain.

Not merely this, but to the connoisseur who believes that Corot, Rousseau, or Millet touched the highest point of painting, these impressionists are intruders, "they come in unbidden; they are ribald when they are not absurd." It is the same old fight between authority and youth, between the individual and the mass. "We do not welcome change, we conservatives. It discredits our masters and confuses us with regard to works we have considered to be mountain-peaks of endeavor."

As a matter of fact, they are justified in taking a serious view of the situation. The change in method indicated by vivid and fearless coloring, indicates a radical change in attitude toward the physical universe. It stands for an advance in the perceptive power of the human eye. Mercifully, for youth, the world of human kind and physical nature forever offers new phases for discovery, for a new work of art; just as new subtleties of force lure minds like Edison's into the shadow, so to the young and unfettered artists new worlds of art beckon.

Let the critic who thinks this a vogue or fad, this impressionist view of nature, beware. It is a discovery, born of clearer vision and more careful study, — a perception which was denied the early painters, precisely as the force we call electricity was an ungovernable power a generation ago.

The dead must give way to the living. It may be sad, but it is the inexorable law, and the veritist and the impressionist will try to submit gracefully to the method of the iconoclasts who shall come when they in their turn are old and sad.

For the impressionists rank themselves with those who believe the final word will never be spoken upon art. That they have added a new word to painting, no competent critic will deny. It has made nature more radiantly beautiful, this new word. Like the word of a lover, it has exalted the painter to see nature irradiated with splendor never seen before. Wherever it is most originally worked out, it makes use of a fundamental principle in an individual way, and it has brought painting abreast of the unprejudiced perception of the lover of nature. The principle is as broad as air, its working out should be individual.

X

LITERARY CENTRES

X. LITERARY CENTRES

A favorite proposition with the business-man of the West is this: "If the West had been settled first, the East would be a wilderness to-day, for the reason (as he goes on to explain) that the fertile soil, the vast cities, the ease of communication of the midland, would have made it the home of all ease, refinement, culture, and art. The East would have been only a fringe of seaport towns, with fine shooting and fishing lands as a background."

If he happens to be a business-man with an imagination (there are such), he will then say: "The East has therefore had its day as a commercial centre. The West has finally been discovered. The East has poured its millions of men and money into the Mississippi valley, and these millions of men have taken root in the soil; and to-day, in the year of 1894, the commercial dominance of the East is distinctly on the wane. Henceforth, the centre of commercial activity in the United States is to be the West. Henceforth, when men of the Old World speak of America, they will not think of Boston and New York and Philadelphia, they will mean Chicago and the Mississippi valley."

There is, of course, an element of exaggeration in this, but there is also in it a larger truth and a magnificent enthusiasm, — an enthusiasm which rises above commercial considerations. The man who really dares to face the future, — and, of course, the man who dares to face the future is he who finds his interests served by it, — the man who can sit down and think of the on-coming millions of the great Mississippi valley, must admit that over-statement of its importance is quite impossible, given time enough for fulfilment.

Commercially, the West rushes toward the future. Cities rise with velocity hitherto inconceivable. True, they are mushrooms to some extent, and are founded upon greed and speculation to a sorrowful extent; but the people are coming on after all, people of higher wisdom and purer life, who will make these mushroom cities temples to art and song. This great basin, like Egypt, like Germany, is to be a "well of nations." It will continually revivify and reinvigorate the East, the extreme North, and the extreme South. It will be the base of food supply; the heart of the nation; the place of interchange.

This leads me to a proposition, which I make on my own account. Literary horizons also are changing with almost equal swiftness. Centres of art production are moving westward; that is to say, the literary supremacy of the East is passing away. There are other and subtler causes than commercial elements at work. Racial influences are at work, and changes in literary and social ideals are hastening a far-reaching subdivision, if not decentralization, of power.

In the West there is coming into expression and literary influence the great Scandinavian and Germanic element to which the traditions of English literature are very weak and unimportant, and to whom Boston and New York are of small account. They have their own race-traditions which neutralize those of the English language which they speak, and thus their minds are left free to choose the most modern things. It is impossible for them to take on the literary traditions of their adopted tongue with equal power, and they find their own less binding by change.

Again, literary traditions are weakening all along the line. The old is passing away, the new is coming on. As the old fades away, the strongholds of tradition and classic interest are forgotten and left behind. This mighty change is a silent one, but it is irresistible. This can be illustrated in the change which has swept over Boston, Concord, and Cambridge during the last ten or twenty years.

Boston has claimed and held supremacy in American literature for more than half a century. Made illustrious by Emerson, Hawthorne, Whittier, Longfellow, Holmes, Lowell, the New England group, it easily kept its place as the most important literary centre in America. New York was second, and Philadelphia third. This Cambridge group has been called "the polite group" and "the Library group." Its members took things for the most part at second hand. They read many books, and mainly wrote gentle and polite poems on books and events. Whittier and Hawthorne, notwithstanding their larger originality, were, after all, related. They took things in a bookish way. It would be absurd to say they were weak or poor, they were very high and noble; but they belonged to another period. They were more closely allied with the past, with English traditions, than we, and were actuated by different ideals of life.

So long as this group lived, Boston was the literary autocrat of the nation. But the school of book-poets is losing power. And, with the change in literary creed, Boston has lost its high place, and it is but natural that she should now take a rather mournful view of American literature.

New York to-day claims to be, and is, the literary centre of America. Boston artists one by one go to New York. Literary men find their market growing there, and dying out in Boston. They find quicker and warmer appreciation in New York, and the critical atmosphere more hospitable. The present receives a larger share of attention than in Boston. Henceforward New York, and not Boston, is to be the great dictator of American literature. New York already assumes to be able to make or break a novelist or playwright. Certainly it is the centre of magazine production; and the magazine is, on the whole, the greatest outlet for distinctive American art.

We are more American in our illustrating and in our fiction than in any other lines of artistic work. New York is the centre of oil-painting as well as of illustration, and its markets exceed those of almost all other American cities taken together. In short, its supremacy in art must be conceded to be as complete to-day as its commercial domination in railways and stocks.

And yet New York is in danger of assuming too much. She must not forget that the writers and painters who make her illustrious are very largely products of the South and West. One needs but to run over the list of the leading magazine-writers of the last ten years, to see how true this is. Ohio sends William D. Howells; Virginia sends Thomas Nelson Page and Amélie Rives; Indiana sends Edward Eggleston, James Whitcomb Riley, Mrs. Catherwood. Tennessee is represented by the Murfree sisters.[1] Georgia, by

---

[1] Garland includes Mary Noailles Murfree's less well-known sister, Fanny Noailles Dickinson Murfree, who published a novel, *Felicia* (1891).

Joel Harris and Richard Malcolm Johnston. Louisiana finds voice through George W. Cable and Ruth McEnnery [sic] Stuart. Arkansas and Kentucky are represented by Alice French and James Lane Allen; and so through a notable list. These are but a few of the best known of the names. Thus, every part of the West or South is represented in the literary domination of New York.

It is not so much a victory of New York over Boston, it is the rising to literary power of the whole nation. New York is but the trumpet through which the whole nation is at last speaking. Let New York remember this and be humble, for the same causes that have cut away the pride of Boston will certainly bring about a corresponding change in the relation of New York to the South and West.

It was easy for Boston to maintain her literary supremacy while the whole population of the nation was less than forty millions, when the whole West was a frontier, and the South was a slave-country. It will be hard for New York to retain her present supremacy with a nation of seventy millions of people, with cities containing half a million people springing up in the interior and on the Western sea, — not to mention Chicago, whose shadow already menaces New York.

Already Chicago claims to have pushed New York from her seat as ruler of our commerce. The whole West and South are in open rebellion against her financial rule. Chicago equals, possibly outnumbers her, in population, and certainly outspeeds her in enterprise. The rise of Chicago as a literary and art centre is a question only of time, and of a very short time; for the Columbian Exposition has taught her her own capabilities in something higher than business. The founding of vast libraries and universities and art museums is the first formal step, the preparation-stage; expression will follow swiftly. Magazines and publishing-houses are to come.

The writers have already risen. Every literary man must have a beginning somewhere, and there are scores of original young writers and artists just rising to power in the West. They need only a channel for utterance; it will come, and they will speak.

It is not contended that the names quoted above are the best, — that they represent the perfect art of the new school. Most of them are young writers, all of them are significant of things to come, but many of them are already of national, even international, fame. The absolutist in his sneer at the rising young artists forgets that the literary masters he worships were once as helpless to reply to the question: What have you done?

It is not intended to say that New York has not her native share in this new movement; I aim merely to show that never again can a city or a group of States overshadow the whole of literary America. It is not merely a question of New York and Chicago now, it is the rise of literary centres all over the nation. Henceforth, St. Louis, New Orleans, Atlanta, Denver, San Francisco, Cincinnati, St. Paul, and Minneapolis, and a dozen more interior cities are to be reckoned with.

Like Avignon and Marseilles, they will have literary men and literary judgments of their own. The process is one of decentralization, together with one of unification.

Never again will any city dominate American literature; and, in my judgment, there will be no over-topping personalities in art. The average is rising; the peaks will seem to sink.

There are other reasons for the revolt against the domination of the East over the whole nation. New York, like Boston, is too near London. It is no longer American. It is losing touch with the people. Chicago is much more American, notwithstanding its foreign population. Its dominant population is splendidly American, drawn from the immediate States, — Indiana, Illinois, Iowa, Wisconsin, Kentucky, and Ohio. It does not profess to be exclusive; it professes to be a meeting-place. Of course, it has its tremulous and timid imitators of New York and Boston imitations of London and Paris; but these people are in a sad minority. The great body of men and women who give strength and originality to Chicago are people who care very little what New York thinks of their work, and the doings of London and Paris are not more vital.

No critic whose eyes are not fastened upon the past can imagine a hopeless literary future for this great nation. To the conservative, who thinks change necessarily destructive and hopeless, the future is a blank. To the radical, who feels change to be necessary and natural, the present and the future are filled with magnificent promise. The horizon widens each year, including more cities, more writers, more lovers of light and song, more makers of literature. Literary invention is as inevitable as the manipulation of the material universe. The material always subtends the intellectual.

Activity in material comes ultimately to be expressed, and expression is commensurate with the deed.

"Bigness does not count," the East says in answer to the West. Yes, but it does! The prairies lead to general conceptions. The winds give strength and penetration and alertness. The mighty stretches of woods lead to breadth and generosity of intellectual conception. The West and South are coming to be something more than big, coming to the expression of a new world, coming to take their places in the world of literature, as in the world of action, and no sneer from gloomy prophets of the dying past can check or chill them.

The literature which is already springing up in those great interior spaces of the South and West is to be a literature, not of books, but of life. It will draw its inspiration from original contact with men and with nature. It will have at first the rough-hewn quality of first-hand work. It is to out-run the old-world limitations.

Its vitalizing element will be its difference of treatment, which will not be that of any other literature of any other place or time, and it is extremely improbable that it will ever submit to any central academy, whether in New York or Chicago.

This school will be one where most notably the individuality of each writer will be respected, and this forbids strict conformity to accepted models. When life is the model and truth the criterion and individualism the coloring element of a literature, the central academy has small power. There will be association as of equals, not slavish acceptance of dictation.

Then again, hero-worship in literature is weakening. In the days when there were few literary men, and these few men professedly held strange powers entirely distinct from their fellows, something of awe went with the reader's admiration. To-day, when the ranks of the poets are thick with adepts, and when the novelists write of comprehensible subjects and lay no claim to mystic power, both poet and novelist are approached without ceremony. This also weakens the hold of the central academy.

The blight upon the literature of the West, like that of all provinces, has been its timidity, its tendency to work in accepted modes, its childish desire to write for the applause of its masters in the East. This has been, in fact, the weakness of the entire output of American literature. The West only emphasizes the fact. In material things, America has boundless self-assertion, but in the arts it has imitated because of its failure to perceive its proper relation to the literature of the world. The West, reckoning itself an annex of the East, has imitated imitations.

Because the East considered itself English in general character, the West, so far as most of its writers are concerned, has acquiesced. As a matter of fact, the West is not English. The Northwest is more largely Teutonic and Scandinavian, and the people of Indiana, Ohio, and Illinois are far removed from England and from English conceptions of life; and this distance is sure to find its statement in literature. Wisconsin, Iowa, Minnesota, Dakota, and other Western States are half composed of men and women of Germanic or Scandinavian extraction. The literature rising from these people will not be English. It will be something new; it will be, and ought to be, American, — that is to say, a new composite.

The centre of this literature of national scope, therefore, cannot be in the East. It will not be dominated by the English idea. It will have no reference to Tennyson or Longfellow or Arnold. Its reference to the north of Europe, to Norway or Germany, will have less of benumbing effect, for these northern peoples are not so deeply enslaved to the past as England is.

The West should work in accordance with the fundamental principles of good writing; that is, it should seek to attain the most perfect lucidity, expressiveness, flexibility, and grace. Its technique should be comprehensible, clear in outline, and infinitely suggestive, ready to be submitted to the world, but free to use new forms.

The choice of subject and the quality which enters into it, like a subtle flavor into wine, should be individual, not subject to any school or master.

The judgment of the East should take rank merely among other judgments; it should not be held all-important.

The purpose of this writing is not merely to combat literary centralization, but also to build up local centres. Wherever a human soul is moved by genuine love of nature and of men to the conscientious and faithful study of the expression of his emotions, there is a literary centre. Around him are grouped minds whose candid criticism can aid and direct him; but this criticism must not evade, nor demand conformity to tradition; it must demand of the young writer truth, sincerity, and individuality.

Let the critics of the local centres remember Mistral and

Whitcomb Riley, who won their way among the people before the critical journals would take count of them. It is the man who has no knowledge of accepted forms, and who therefore refers every work of art back to nature, who is quickest to respond to the literature of life. The average American is quick to thrill to real emotion, only he wants it direct and unaffected.

I believe in the local magazine. With the growth of inland cities in wealth and refinement, the magazine will come to displace the mere newspaper, possibly the newspaper will grow into the magazine. The work of the local magazines like "The Southern," "The Californian," "The Midland," "The Overland," can be made of vast importance in the nation's life.[2]

Let them keep close to the local life, developing the best — that is, the simplest and most natural — talent of their region, making their appeal constantly to the unspoiled yet discerning taste of the middle-conditioned people, and they will succeed. "They have always failed in the past," says the doubter; possibly, but the past is not the present or the future. Taste is rising. Culture is broadening swiftly. A new generation is coming on, — a generation of veritists. Con-

[2] "The Southern" could be a short title for several magazines, but Garland probably means *The Southern Review* (1869–1879), edited by Albert Taylor Bledsoe and published for the most part at Baltimore. This magazine was particularly distinguished in its literary content. "The Californian" is probably *The Californian Illustrated Magazine* (1891–1894), edited by Charles Frederick Holder and published at San Francisco. *The Midland* (1894–1898), edited and published in Des Moines, Iowa, by Johnson Brigham was the literary magazine of Iowa in the nineties. Garland contributed to its first issue. *The Overland* (1865–1875; 1883–1933?) was published in San Francisco and, during its first two and one-half years, edited by Bret Harte.

ditions grow more hospitable to this local literature with great rapidity. What was true of local conditions five years ago will scarcely be true to-day.

O Sayers and Doers of this broad, free inland America of ours! to you is given the privilege of being broad and free in your life and letters. You should not be bound to a false and dying culture, you should not endeavor to re-enact the harsh and fierce and false social dramas of the Old World. You should not turn your face to the east, to the past. Your comment should be that of free men and women, loving equality, justice, truth.

Yours not to worship crumbling idols; your privilege and pleasure should be to face life and the material earth in a new way, — moulding old forms of government into new shapes, catching from earth and sea and air, new songs to sing, new thoughts to frame, new deeds to dare.

XI

LITERARY MASTERS

XI. LITERARY MASTERS

It is all a question of masters. There are masters who set free, there are masters who enslave. The best critic is he who frees, and the best criticism of the Old World has demanded of America, not imitations of the old forms, but free, faithful, characteristic work. It is the second-class critic who enslaves to the past, unable to comprehend advance.

For fifty years the best critics of England and of Europe have been calling for the native utterance of American writers. Posnett, Dowden, Taine, Véron, Freiligrath, Björnson, every critic who has perceived the forward movement of all art, has looked for a new conception, a new flavor, a new manner in American literature; and almost as constantly have the conservative and narrow critics of Boston and New York discouraged the truest, freest, utterance of the American poet and novelist. Not all have been of this hopeless type, but it remains true as a general comment. Upon the tender springing plant of American literature the frost of conservative culture has ever fallen. No wonder the young writer has turned to copying old forms, and so benumbed and sterilized his creative soul.

It really comes down to a contest, *not between the East and the West, but between sterile culture and creative work; between mere scholarship and wisdom; between conservative criticism and native original literary production.*

It is a question of books *versus* a literature of life, a struggle between adaption [sic] to new surroundings and conformity to the ancestral type. It is only because there happen to be more conservatives in the East that the contest takes on the appearance of a war between East and West.

The East has its magnificent radicals, men who stand for free art and modern art. I do not forget the encouragement which the young writer owes to them; and yet these Eastern radicals will be the first to acknowledge the truth I write concerning the dangers of a centralization of power.

Shall our literature be a literature of the East, in mode if not in subject, or shall it be national? Is it to be only so large as the conception of New York and Boston critics, or shall it be as big and broad and democratic as the best thought of the whole nation? Is every work of art of every Western or Southern man or woman to be submitted with timid air to a jury that represents only a section of American society, — a section which is really nearer the Old World than the New, — or shall the writing be addressed to the whole nation? Is it safe to depend upon a half-dozen publishing houses, or a half-dozen magazines, for outlet? Would it not be better to have many magazines, provided, of course, the standard of excellence were high? Editors and critics are human. They are likely, at best, to be biassed by their personal likes and dislikes. It is not well that too much power be vested in any one city.

The supposition is that America finds amplest outlet in its present magazines, which are mainly in the East; but this is not true. It is a physical impossibility first; and, second, the theory is that the magazines are conducted for Eastern readers and in harmony with the traditions inherited by the East.

This is not complaint. No young writer of to-day has less cause for complaint than I. It is a statement of fact. There have arisen in the East these great magazines, hospitable in their way, but limited and inadequate to the expression of the art-life of this great nation. Their influence has been beneficent, — is yet; but there is a greater, truer, and freer expression of this people which will come only with the rise of native inland magazines.

As a matter of fact, this controversy is not sectional. It is in the East as well as in the West. All over America, in towns and cities, there are groups of readers whom our reigning monthlies do not represent. These readers have not only all the substantial acquirements of the conservatives, but possess a broader Americanism and a more intimate knowledge of American life than the aristocrat who prides himself on never having been farther west than Buffalo.

The culture represented by these radicals is not alone based upon knowledge of dead forms of art; it includes living issues of art. The number of these readers increases year by year. They stand for ideas and conditions of the future, and from them artists are rising, filled with courage and moved by convictions of their allegiance to truth. These people demand something more than smooth conventional work. They realize the tendency of young authors not to write as they really feel, but as they think the editors of the great magazines would have them write. They realize the danger which lies in putting into the hands of a few men, no matter how fine they may be, the directing power of American literature.

These cultivated and fearless radicals join Western readers in saying, "By what right do you of the conservative East assume to be final judges of American literature? What special qualifications does a residence on the extreme eastern shore of our nation give you, by which to settle all questions of a national literature?"

"The West is crude," Eastern critics are fond of saying.

"What do you mean by that? Do you mean that there are not men and women of the highest type in the West? Do you mean that we do not conform to your specific ideal of culture? Or do you mean that we have not been self-respecting enough in our own thinking? In what lies your assumed superiority over the West?"

To this the East replies: "We are the occupying claimants of the glory of the great men of this century's literature. We have also the great libraries, the museums, the great universities, which makes us the centre of critical intelligence. Granting your great railways, your stupendous enterprises, your great cities, the East still remains, and must remain, the centre of the highest literary culture in America."

The West rejoins: "That is precisely the point at issue. We deny that the East is to be the exclusive home of the broadest culture. We feel that much of this culture is barren and insincere. It has a hopeless outlook. It leads nowhere. It treads a circle, like the logic of the Koran.

"Culture is not creative power. Scholarship does not imply wisdom. We do not believe a city at our farthest East can remain the city most progressive in its art, most unbiassed in its judgment. The American city of broadest culture is henceforth to be that where the broad, free currents of American life daily ebb and flow. Such a city can know and will know all that the East knows of fundamental principles of art and literature, and will have a wider knowledge of the scope and action of American life."

The conservative of the East then says: "It will take a hundred years to make a Western city into the likeness of New York or Boston. The mellow charm of our literary atmosphere is the growth of two centuries. Our very streets are lined with suggestive walls and historical tablets. Our drawing-rooms and our clubs represent the flowering culture of ten generations."

The West quickly responds: "Keep your past. Hug your tablets to your bosom: you are welcome to all that; we are concerned with the present, and with the splendor of the future. Your culture is too largely of the moribund. Cleverness will not save you. You fail to conceive that our idea of culture is a different and, we assert, a higher form, because it refers to a culture of living forms. Besides, culture, even of the broadest, is only part of it; creative power is the crowning splendor of a nation's life. Scholarship does not necessarily imply wisdom. The study of the past does little for original genius. Libraries and universities produce few of the great leaders of American thought; all that books can give is our inheritance as well as yours."

The radical continues: "We deny that the Eastern 'art atmosphere' is necessary to the production of original works of art. We doubt the ability of New York or Boston criticism to pass final judgment upon a Western work of art, because the conditions of our life are outside the circle of its intimate knowledge. A criticism which stands for old things, we repeat, is not the criticism which is to aid the production of characteristic American art. America is not to submit itself to the past; it is to be free."

"Do you mean to say that you propose to cut loose from the past?" asks the traditionalist.

"By no means. We expect to assert our right to our day, as Russia, Norway, Germany, and others of our neighbor nations have done. The youth of all nations are in the fight. We are in the midst of one of those returning cycles of progress in art when the young man attains his majority. America has begun to attain her majority, to claim the right to a free choice in art as well as in government, to speak her own mind in her own way."

"Permit us — are you to use as a medium, Choctaw or English?" the East inquires, in strenuously polite phrase.

"That illustrates the inadequateness and the illiberality of your attitude toward us. We propose to use the speech of living men and women. We are to use actual speech as we hear it and to record its changes. We are to treat of the town and city as well as of the farm, each in its place and through the medium of characteristic speech. We propose to discard your nipping accent, your nice phrases, your balanced sentences, and your neat proprieties inherited from the eighteenth century. Our speech is to be as individual as our view of life."

The conservative replies: "Your view of life is of no interest to us. We do not see the necessity of Americans troubling to write or paint at all in future. We have books and paintings enough in the market. When we want a book, we buy a classic, and know what we are getting. When we

want a painting, there are Corots and Rousseaus and Bou-
guereaus in the markets. Produce wheat and corn and rail-
way-stocks yet awhile, and don't trouble yourself about
literary problems. Read the classics for the improvement of
your style. In the mean time, we will see that American
literature is not vulgarized."

The Western radical warmly replies: "Who constituted
you the guardian of American literature? What do you
know of the needs or tastes of the people — "

Testily the aristocrat breaks in: "My dear sir, I care nothing for any tastes but my own. I don't like the common
American in life, and I don't like him in books. Therefore—"

"There!" rejoins the radical, triumphantly. "There is a
second point admitted. You have no sympathy with the
American people of middle condition. You are essentially
aristocratic and un-American in your position. From your
library, or from the car-window, you look upon our life;
that is the extent of your knowledge of our conditions, at
best. For the most part you have never been west of Niagara
Falls. How can you be just to this literature which springs
from a life you do not know or sympathize with?

"We are forming a literature from direct contact with
life, and such a literature can be estimated only by unbiassed minds and by comparison with nature and the life
we live. Are you fitted to be the court of last resort upon
our writing by reason of your study of English novels and
your study of last-century painting? The test of a work of
art is not, Does it conform to the best models? but, *Does it
touch and lift and exalt men?* And we profess ability to perceive these qualities even west of the Mississippi River.

"We care little for the free-masonry of literary phrases which relates one spectacled enthusiast over dead men's books to a similar devotee of dead men's pictures. The West should aim to be wise rather than cultured. Wisdom is democratic, culture is an aristocrat. Wisdom is knowledge of principle, culture is a knowledge of forms and accepted conditions; the contention is world old, but necessary."

In the above colloquy, which may be typical in a measurable degree, I have put the Western radical over against the Eastern conservative, not because there are not conservatives in the West and radicals in the East, but because it is my sincere conviction, taking the largest view, that the interior is to be henceforth the real America. From these interior spaces of the South and West the most vivid and fearless and original utterance of the coming American democracy will come.

This is my conviction. I might adduce arguments based on the difference in races; I might speculate upon the influence of the Irish and Jews and Italians upon New York and Boston, and point out the quicker assimilation of the Teutonic races in the West, but it would only be passed over by the reader.

I confess to a certain failure to adequately portray what I mean. The things I would put in evidence are intangible. There are the mighty spaces of the West, the swarming millions of young men and women coming on in this empire of the Mississippi valley. Some imaginative Easterners caught glimpses of it at the Exposition, where the Eastern culture and accent was swallowed up and lost in the mighty flood of the middle West, unknown and inarticulate, but tremendous in its mass.

It is impossible to convey to others the immense faith in this land which intimate knowledge, gained by fifty thousand miles of travel, has built up in me. I know my West; I know its young minds. I can see their eager faces before me as I write. I know the throb of creative force everywhere thrilling the young men and women of these States, and yet I realize my inability to put it in evidence. I might mention names, writers of whose power I am assured, — they would be unknown; circumstances may crush them.

America is the most imaginative and creative of nations. Its inventions, its huge constructions, prove that. Only in its literature and art has it been bound by tradition. Its inventive and its original constructive genius arose from needs which dominated tradition. Its great railways, bridges, tunnels, transportation facilities, were perfected by minds which rose out of the common ranks of American life. The genuine American literature, in the same way, must come from the soil and the open air, and be likewise freed from tradition. Such an epoch is upon us.

Lowell felt this, in spite of his English environment. In his old age something of his early faith in America came back to him.[1]

"No: morning and the dewy prime are born into the earth again with every child. It is our fault if drouth and dust usurp the noon. . . . Our time is not an unpoetic one. This lesson I learn from the

[1] Garland implies that this statement is from Lowell's later life. Actually it is from an early speech, never published by Lowell, which appeared with a prefatory note by Charles Eliot Norton in the *Century Magazine*, XLVII, 3 (Jan. 1894), 432–439. The passage quoted is on p. 439.

past: that grace and goodness, the fair, the noble, and the true will never cease out of the world till the God from whom they emanate ceases out of it. . . . Lives of the great poets teach us they were the men of their generation who felt most deeply the meaning of the present."

XII

A RECAPITULATORY
AFTER-WORD

XII. A RECAPITULATORY AFTER-WORD

There come times in the development of every art when the creative mind re-asserts itself, and shakes itself loose from the terrible power of the past. This dissent, this demand for artistic freedom, is always made by youth, and always meets with the bitter and scornful opposition of the old. To conform is easy, — it is like sleep. To dissent is action in the interests of the minority.

At certain times a great writer like Dante or Shakespeare or Hugo or Ibsen rises, — a grand innovator and dissenter, — and holds intellectual dominion over the world during his life, apparently by his personal force and expression; and after his death, critics who draw their rules of art from him come to worship and bow down before him as a demigod of literature. He becomes a fetich.

Once an author reaches this stage, he becomes an incubus. His personal defects are exalted into universal excellencies, methods to be copied. He becomes the standard of measurement for the critic without discernment or judgment of his own. It is so easy to say of the new artist, "He paints purple shadows on the snow; Corot did not, therefore the young artist is wrong." Of such is the criticism based upon past models.

Meanwhile, Shakespeare and Corot are innocent of this. Were Corot living to-day, he would be in the advance line of present art. Shakespeare would be grappling with present themes, like the tremendous iconoclast he was. Burns would be a social radical and a writer of modern dialect.

These men rebelled against authority in their day. They did not dream of becoming obstructing authorities after their death.

As a matter of fact, literary power is not personal; it is at bottom sociologic. The power of the writer is derived from the society in which he lives; like the power of a general, which springs from the obedience of his army. When society changes, when his audience dies, the writer's power passes away. This is the natural law, and would take way easily and quickly were there not other tendencies to conserve and retard, just as in the animal organisms.

Schools are conservative forces. They are nearly always linked with the aristocratic and the old, especially in their art instructions. Universities are bulwarks of tradition. They are pools left on the beach by an ebbing tide. They conserve the past. They study the living present but little. They are founded upon books. They teach conformity, they do not develop personality.

The natural thing for our society to-day is to demand of its artists fresh and vivid interpretations of nature and society. The feudalistic forms of life are drawing off. The certainly democratic is coming on. It is natural for Americans to say: Sophocles, Shakespeare, Molière, Schiller do not satisfy us. They represent other outlooks upon life. They do not touch us directly. We prefer a more human and sympathetic art, — something nearer and sweeter.

This, I repeat, is the natural feeling of the ordinary man or woman of to-day, and yet such has been the power of the conservative forces in art that the dissenter acquiesced in outer expression while privately throwing his Shake-

speare aside for Dickens, George Eliot, Hugo, and Tur-
genief. He has applauded the orator who said "Shakespeare
ended the drama;" but he has left Shakespeare to gather
dust on his library walls while he reads the newspaper and
meets his friends in conversation about the latest comic
opera. In other words, literary hypocrites are made plenti-
ful by the pressure of conservative criticism precisely as in
the religious world.

The quality most needed in literary discussion to-day is
not learning, it is candor. Literary discussion is full of lies.
Men profess to admire things which do not touch them.
They uphold forms of art which they know to be dead.
They fear to be called destructionists. They feel in some
way bound to lie for the sake of youth. Youth must be
dulled into a literary hypocrite, and so all mouths are set
awry.

But an era of reorganization is upon us. The common
man is again moving in intellectual unrest, as in the time
of Burns and Shelley. The young men are to speak their
minds. The re-assertion of artistic independence is to be
made. The literary fetich is to fail of power, and original
genius once more push the standards of art forward.

As a matter of fact, old idols are crumbling in literature
and painting as in religion. "Changeless throughout the
centuries, they sit upon their inapproachable thrones," cries
the rhetorician; but it is only a fine figure of speech. As a
matter of fact, they are being worn away. An impalpable
sand, blown upon them by ceaseless winds from free
spaces, has worn them down; their blurred features wear
a look of vague appeal. They are no longer as gods!

Below them the changing currents of human life, grown quicker, pass by without looking up there where they sit. Great seams are opening in the base of their thrones; they will soon fall, these few remaining ones, as all the others have fallen, and the rivers of life will pass by on the other side.

That this should happen seems dreadful and impossible to the conservative mind; to the dissenter, it is in conformity with the great law of evolution. The dynamic conception of art does not mourn over decay; it faces the on-coming day, content to be and to do, now.

"Æschylus, there he lies, deep in the past, a colossal fragment, his brow projecting above the sands of centuries," cries Hugo.[1] Yes, there he lies, and there Shakespeare lies, sunk and sinking, just as every other human soul sinks into the sand. In the illimitable sweep of the centuries there is little to choose between a reign of two centuries and one of fifty years.

In the carcass of every dead lion, maggots breed and fatten, unmindful of the green grass and the fresh wind blowing by, hearing not the living lion's royal tread. So the scholiast bores and bores in the dead body of the past; his sluggish sense dead to the smell of growing corn and the moving by of living things.

Not from such sources does a living literature flow. Each age of strong creative capability reveals life in its own fashion; that is, each creative age in the past uttered its own truth as over against the conventionalized dogmas of its teachers. I believe such a period of literary breaking-

[1] Cf. Victor Hugo, *William Shakespeare* (Paris, 1864), pp. 110–111.

away has come in America. Whitman announced it, but could not exemplify it in popular form. He voiced its force, its love of liberty and love of comrades, but he was the prophet, not the exemplar. He said well, that the real literature of America could not be a polite literature. The nation is too great, too sincere.

There is coming in this land the mightiest assertion in art of the rights of man and the glory of the physical universe ever made in the world. It will be done, not by one man, but by many men and women. It will be born, not of drawing-room culture, nor of imitation, nor of fear of masters, nor will it come from homes of great wealth. It will come from the average American home, in the city as well as in the country. It will deal with all kinds and conditions. It will be born of the mingling seas of men in the vast interior of America, because there the problem of the perpetuity of our democracy, the question of the liberty as well as the nationality of our art, will be fought out. This literature will be too great to submit to the domination of any literary centre or literary master. With cities of a half a million inhabitants, scattered from Pittsburg to Seattle, New York and Chicago will alike be made humble.

Rise, O young man and woman of America! Stand erect! Face the future with a song on your lips and the light of a broader day in your eyes. Turn your back on the past, not in scorn, but in justice to the future. Cease trying to be correct, and become creative. This is our day. The past is not vital. It is a highway of dust, and Homer, Æschylus, Sophocles, Dante, Shakespeare are milestones. Libraries do not create great poets and artists; they seldom aid, and they often warp and destroy them. To know Shakespeare is good. To know your fellow-men is better. All that Shakespeare knew of human life, you may know, but not at second hand, not through Shakespeare, not through the eyes of the dead, but at first hand.

In evolution there are always two vast fundamental forces: one, the inner, which propels; the other, the outer, which adapts and checks. One forever thrusts toward new forms, the other forever moulds, conserves, adapts, reproduces. Progress is the resultant of these forces.

The force that flowers is the individual, that which checks and moulds is environment. Impulse is the stronger to-day, tomorrow conformity chills and benumbs. Of such cycles is the history of art. Rebellious youth breaks from the grim hand of the past and toils in his own way till he grows old, and then becomes oppressor in his turn; and death again liberates youth, whose keen nostril breathes again the air of heaven as if the centuries had been clock-ticks.

Of what avail then, O you of the dead past!

What fear ye, O youth, to whom life smells so sweet! Accept the battle challenge cheerfully, as those before you have done. What you win, you must fight for as of old. And remember, life and death both fight with you. Idols crumble and fall, but the skies lift their unmoved arch of blue, and the earth sends forth is rhythmic pulse of green, and in the blood of youth there comes the fever of rebellious art.

BIOGRAPHICAL GLOSSARY

BIOGRAPHICAL GLOSSARY

Allen, James Lane (1849–1925), author of local color stories of Kentucky, among them *Flute and Violin* (1891).

Barlow, Jane (1857–1917), Irish poet, critic, and chronicler of peasant life, whose *Irish Idylls* (1892) was modelled on Barrie's studies of Scotland.

Barlow, Joel (1754–1812), American author of an epic, *The Vision of Columbus* (1787), and a mock-epic, *The Hasty Pudding* (1796).

Barrie, James M. (1860–1937), British dramatist and novelist, whose *A Window in Thrums* (1889) was set in his native Scotland.

Benson, Frank Weston (1862–1951), American painter and etcher.

Bird, Robert Montgomery (1806–1854), American author of romances, among them *Nick of the Woods: or the Jibbenainosay* (1837). Bird also wrote plays and revised *Metamora* for his friend Edwin Forrest.

Björnson, Björnstjerne (1832–1910), Norwegian poet, novelist, and dramatist. An ardent nationalist, Björnson wrote *folke-stykker* to create "a new saga in the light of the peasant."

Bunker, Dennis M. (1861–1890), American painter, specialized in portraits of women and figure paintings.

Cable, George Washington (1844–1925), author of Louisiana local-color stories, among them *The Grandissimes* (1880).

Catherwood, Mary Hartwell (1847–1902), author of historical romances. Mrs. Catherwood opposed Garland in a debate on realism at the time of the Chicago World's Fair.

Colton, George Hooker (1818–1847), author of a dramatic poem, *Tecumseh: or The West Thirty Years Since* (1842).

Corot, Camille Jean Baptiste (1896–1875), French painter.

Dagnan-Bouveret (1852–1929), French painter, many of whose early subjects were the peasants of Brittany.

Davis, Richard Harding (1864–1916), American novelist and journalist. Davis also wrote many plays, some of them dramatizations of his own stories.

Detaille, Jean Baptiste Edouard (1848–1912), French painter known for the precision and detail of his work.

Diaz de la Peña, Narcisse Virgile (1809–1876), French landscape painter.

Dowden, Edward (1843–1913), Irish scholar and critic. For his view of American letters, see the essay, "The Poetry of Democracy: Walt Whitman," in his *Studies in Literature, 1789–1877* (London, 1882).

Eggleston, Edward (1837-1902), Indiana novelist best known for *The Hoosier Schoolmaster* (1871).

Enneking, John (1841–1916), New England landscape painter. Enneking's estimate of the market for his work resembles Garland's view of the demand for local color: "I paint portraits of places, scenes people know and love, and put a price on them people can pay. The average man likes to recognize something familiar in a painting." Quoted in Hamlin Garland, *Roadside Meetings* (N.Y., 1930), p. 27.

Fitch, Clyde (1865–1909), American playwright. His serious studies of contemporary society include *A Modern Match* (1892) and *The Climbers* (1901).

Frederic, Harold (1856–1898), New York author whose novels, *Seth's Brother's Wife* (1887) and *The Lawton Girl* (1890), depict contemporary life in New York state.

Freiligrath, Herman Ferdinand (1810–1876), German poet who translated Whitman and Bret Harte.

French, Alice (1850–1934), local color writer of Arkansas and Iowa.

Harrigan, Edward (1845–1911), actor and author of plays and dramatic sketches. Harrigan's sketches of the "Mulligan Guard" were inspired by the amateur military societies of the New York Irish.

Harris, Joel Chandler (1848–1908), author of the Uncle Remus tales.

Harte, [Francis] Bret (1836–1902), author of stories of California mining camps, among them *The Luck of Roaring Camp and Other Sketches* (1870).

Hassam, Childe (1859–1935), American impressionist painter.

BIOGRAPHICAL GLOSSARY

Hillhouse, James Abraham (1789–1841), American author of romantic verse dramas.

Inness, George (1825–1894), American landscape painter.

Johnston, Richard Malcomb (1822–1898), author of local color stories, among them *Georgia Sketches* (1864).

Kemeys, Edward (1843–1907), wild-animal sculptor of Chicago.

Kipling, Rudyard (1865–1936), English author whose *Plain Tales From the Hills* (1888) was adapted from stories which introduced the "soldiers three": Ortheris, Mulvaney, and Learoyd.

Kirkland, Joseph (1830–1894), Illinois novelist, author of *Zury: The Meanest Man in Spring County* (1887) and *The McVeys* (1888).

Lanceray, Iévguéni Alesandrovitch (1848–1886), Russian sculptor.

Matthews, [James] Brander (1852–1929). A playwright in the 1880's and 90's, Matthews was professor of dramatic literature at Columbia University, 1900–1924.

MacKnight, Dodge (1860–1950), American painter, specialized in water colors.

Meissonier, Jean Louis Ernest (1815–1891), French painter known for his detailed style.

Miller, Joaquin, pseud. Cincinnatus Hiner (or Heine) Miller (1841?–1913), California poet.

Millet, Jean François (1814–1875), French painter.

Mistral, Frédéric (1830–1914), Provençal poet, a founder of the Félibrige, a society dedicated to encouraging literary works in the dialect of Provence.

Monet, Claude (1840–1926), French impressionist.

Murfree, Mary Noailles (1850–1922), author of local color stories of Tennessee, among them *In the Tennessee Mountains* (1884).

Page, Thomas Nelson (1853–1922), wrote tales of the pre-Civil War South and specialized in the dialect story.

Perry, Lila Cabot (1848–1933), American painter; wife of the critic Thomas Sargent Perry.

Posnett, Hutchinson Macauley (–), English critic.

Read, Opie (1852–1939), local color writer of Kentucky and Arkansas.

Remington, Frederick (1861–1909), American painter and sculptor.

BIOGRAPHICAL GLOSSARY

Riley, James Whitcomb (1849–1916), Indiana poet best known for the series of dialect poems by "Benjamin F. Johnson."

Rives, Amélie (1863–1945), Virginia novelist, poet, and playwright.

Rogers, John (1829–1904), American sculptor whose realistic statuettes depicting homely scenes from contemporary life are known as "Rogers Groups."

Rousseau, Etienne Pierre Théodore (1812–1867), French landscape painter.

Schreiner, Olive Emilie Albertina (1855–1920), South African novelist and essayist whose first book, *The Story of an African Farm* (1883), criticized Christianity and advocated the emancipation of women.

Sinding, Otto Ludvig (1842–1909), Norwegian painter.

Steele, Theodore Clement (1847–1926), American painter whose studies of the Indiana landscape Garland admired.

Stuart, Ruth McEnery (1849–1917), author of Louisiana local color stories depicting the post-bellum South.

Taine, Hippolyte Adolphe (1828–1893), French critic and historian.

Tarbell, Edmund Charles (1862–1939), American painter, a successful member of the artistic circle in Boston.

Thanet, Octave, pseud. Alice French.

Troyon, Constant (1810–1865), French painter of landscape and animals.

Valdes, Armando Palacio (1853–1938), Spanish realistic novelist.

Véron, Eugène (1825–1889), French philosopher and historian.

Webber, Charles Wilkins (1819–1856), author of melodramatic tales of the Wild West.

Wegman, Bertha (1847–1926), Danish painter.

Wilkins, Mary E. (1852–1930), Massachusetts local color writer.

Zorn, Anders (1860–1920), Swedish impressionist painter.

THE JOHN HARVARD LIBRARY

*The intent of
Waldron Phoenix Belknap, Jr.,
as expressed in an early will, was for
Harvard College to use the income from a
permanent trust fund he set up, for "editing and
publishing rare, inaccessible, or hitherto unpublished
source material of interest in connection with the
history, literature, art (including minor and useful
art), commerce, customs, and manners or way of
life of the Colonial and Federal Periods of the United
States . . . In all cases the emphasis shall be on the
presentation of the basic material." A later testament
broadened this statement, but Mr. Belknap's interests remained constant until his death.*

*In linking the name of the first benefactor of
Harvard College with the purpose of this later,
generous-minded believer in American culture the
John Harvard Library seeks to emphasize the importance of Mr. Belknap's purpose. The John Harvard
Library of the Belknap Press of Harvard University
Press exists to make books and documents
about the American past more readily
available to scholars and the
general reader.*